HARDY PERENNIALS
A BEGINNER'S GUIDE

HARDY PERENNIALS

A BEGINNER'S GUIDE

ERIC SAWFORD

GUILD OF MASTER CRAFTSMAN
PUBLICATIONS LTD

First published 2000 by
Guild of Master Craftsman Publications Ltd,
166 High Street, Lewes,
East Sussex, BN7 1XU

ISBN 1 86108 150 2

A catalogue record of this book is available from the British Library

Photographs by Eric Sawford
Illustrations by Katy Sleight

Designed by Joyce Chester
Cover design by Ian Smith, Guild of Master Craftsman Design Studio
Typefaces: Sabon, Frutiger and Lithos
Colour origination by Viscan Graphics (Singapore)
Printed and bound by Kyodo Printing (Singapore) under the supervision of
MRM Graphics, Winslow, Buckinghamshire, UK

CONTENTS

INTRODUCTION

AS I WRITE this introduction, the late-flowering hardy plants are still making a brave show – the colourful Michaelmas daisies are attracting the butterflies, *Rudbeckia* 'Goldsturm' has plenty of its black-centred yellow daisies, and my delightful old favourites, the Japanese anemones, are still in flower. Doubtless, with a high pressure area forecast, a sharp frost one morning in the very near future will bring all of this to an end.

It is reassuring, however, that it will not be long before the first buds of the Christmas rose appear, soon to be followed, if the weather is mild, by the enchanting *Helleborus* Oriental Hybrids, widely known as Lenten rose. This all goes to show that, with a careful choice of species, hardy plants can be in flower for most of the year.

There is a vast number of perennial plants widely available today, in an extensive range of forms, heights and colours. All are container grown, which gives the advantage that they can be planted out, except when the ground is wet or frozen. Having said that, the traditional planting time of autumn or spring is still the best.

Numerous nurserymen specialize in hardy plants, some concentrating on a particular genera; two favourites are hostas and hemerocallis. It is from these outlets that the latest introductions can be obtained, many of which have been raised overseas. Nowadays garden centres carry a wide range of perennials, especially in the spring. These include well-grown, sizable specimens that will flower in the same year. At the other end of the scale are much smaller and cheaper plants that will take a while to reach a size when they are able to produce a display.

This book covers 70 of the best-known perennials, plants that grow and flower year after year, with details of varieties. It is difficult to know what to include, such is the range of hardy subjects available today. Preliminary chapters focus on planting, cultivation, propagation and some of the commonest pests and diseases. There are a number of ways to grow hardy perennials. Top of the list must be as a border, at its finest during the summer months. Space permitting, the fashionable island bed has many advantages; grown in this way, plants seem to require less staking and tying up and there is all-round visibility. In many cases, perennials will be included in a border containing bulbs, grasses and shrubs – an ideal way to grow them.

The plants widely available today are very different from when I started gardening. My memories go back to large clumps of orange daylilies, catmint edging flower beds and great expanses of Shasta daisies.

Currently offered are legions of daylilies in a range of brilliant and pastel colours; other plants mentioned are, of course, still available and doubtless will be for years to come despite the many attractive introductions which appear annually.

A herbaceous border is at its best during the summer, but should contain plants to flower during other seasons

1

PERENNIALS THROUGH THE SEASONS

WITH a well-planned selection of hardy perennials there is likely to be only a few weeks in the garden with little in flower, such is the range widely available. Around the turn of the year the first hellebores flower. Depending on weather conditions, the one most likely to be first off the mark is the well-known Christmas rose, *Helleborus niger*, followed by the Lenten rose, now mostly hybrid strains in a wide range of colours. The greenish flowers of *H. foetidus* may not be to everyone's liking but it is, nevertheless, a good plant for some of the difficult spots, where it can be left undisturbed to keep itself going by self-seeding.

WINTER

If it is a mild winter, several plants will be coming into flower by March, among them epimediums, pulmonarias and various primulas. The hellebores are very useful for late winter/early spring colour, especially the very popular Oriental Hybrids. The well-known drumstick primula, *P. denticulata*, will be at its best in early spring. It is now widely

The hellebores are very useful for providing late winter/early spring colour, especially the very popular Oriental Hybrids

Delphiniums, phlomis and hardy geraniums of several varieties make a colourful show during June

available in several colours and in a lovely pure white form. Invaluable for their bright yellow flowers in early spring are the doronicums, which blend in well with bulbs. One of the best known doronicums is the single-flowered hybrid 'Miss Mason', along with the fully double 'Frühlingspracht'; better known in Britain as 'Spring Beauty', this is another excellent choice.

SPRING AND SUMMER

By June things are really moving in the border, which can become a kaleidoscope of colour at this time. Among those flowering at this time are tall bearded iris, gorgeous paeonies and hardy geraniums in a range of sizes and colours, with many more following as the weeks go by. The summer months are when

The majority of hardy perennials are in full bloom during the summer months. There are numerous, small-flowered hemerocallis suitable for smaller gardens, including 'Meadow Sprite'

BORDER PLAN 1: TO PROVIDE COLOUR FROM

KEY TO BORDER PLAN

1 *Primula* 'Guinevere'

2 *Pulmonaria* 'Cambridge Blue Group'

3 *Sedum spectabile*

4 *Geranium sanguineum*

5 *Aster* 'Veilchenkönigin' ('Violet Queen')

6 *Astilbe chinensis* var. *pumila*

7 *Euphorbia polychroma*

8 *Helleborus* Oriental Hybrids

9 *Alchemilla mollis*

10 Phlox

11 Border iris

12 Phlox

13 Border iris

14 *Anemone hupehensis* (Japanese anemone)

15 *Rudbeckia* 'Goldsturm'

16 *Crocosmia*

17 *Echinacea* 'The King'

18 *Ligularia* 'The Rocket'

19 *Campanula* 'Prichard's Variety'

20 *Kniphofia rooperi*

21 Hemerocallis

EARLY SPRING UNTIL FIRST AUTUMN FROSTS

Position hardy plants with 'hot-coloured' flowers, such as this brilliant red oriental poppy, with care

AUTUMN

By early autumn, most of the early-flowering perennials will be over with many others nearing the end of their display. Fortunately, plants such as *Verbena bonariensis* will still carry on. These hold a great attraction for butterflies, as do the varieties of *Sedum spectabile*, often referred to as ice-plant, some with large, flat heads of pink flowers. Even more eye-catching are the red-flowered 'Brilliant', 'Indian Chief' and 'September Glow', all great favourites with the tortoiseshell butterflies.

the border really comes into its own; stately delphiniums and ligularias are just two of the taller subjects available, with daylilies and richly coloured oriental poppies providing bold splashes of colour.

No perennial border is complete without at least one or two of the ever-popular Michaelmas daisies, which are invaluable for adding colour late in the season. They range from low-growing plants reaching 60cm/24in – ideal for the front of a border – to those reaching 1.5m/5ft or more. Some of the later-flowering varieties will continue to

Always a good choice for its late flowers is *Rudbeckia* 'Goldsturm', which will flower until the first sharp frost brings it to an abrupt end

The autumn months are the best time for Michaelmas daisies and coreopsis, both of which often flower until the first sharp frosts

bloom right up until the first sharp autumn frost, which changes many things in the garden overnight.

One of the best autumn-flowering perennials has to be *Rudbeckia* 'Goldsturm'. This vigorous, free-flowering plant can certainly be relied upon to provide a grand show of deep yellow, black-centred flowers until a frost cuts them back – this is the time to clear up the border and look forward to next year's display.

Having said that, there are many subjects which can be left throughout the winter to add interest to the garden. Examples include evergreen plants which take on attractive winter colouring – there is none better than *Bergenia* 'Bressingham Ruby' – and some of the grasses, which remain attractive having long since turned brown. Of course, do not overlook plants with ornamental seed heads.

Several bergenias take on very attractive winter foliage

2

PREPARING THE BORDER

AUTUMN is an ideal time to start work on a border. Choose an open, well drained location – never one which becomes waterlogged or is overhung by trees. Avoid windy spots as far as possible as such a location will almost certainly result in plants being blown about, or even worse, flattened by summer storms when in flower. Dig over the ground to a depth of 25cm/10in, roughly the length of a spade's blade, turning the soil right over so that what was on top becomes buried. This will kill weeds and expose the lower soil to the weather – during the winter, frost will break down the soil, which makes it easier for planting in the spring. When digging, incorporate as much well-rotted compost, manure or leaf mould as possible. This will improve the soil texture, feed the plants and help to retain moisture.

One of the worst problems to be encountered in a border is that of perennial weeds – these should be removed while digging. Keep a careful watch, as even a small piece of bindweed root will produce a new plant. Other very troublesome subjects are ground elder and couch grass. Here again, remove all pieces seen as you prepare the soil for planting. Annual weeds will germinate; these can be controlled by carefully hoeing around the plants.

Drainage of heavy soils can be improved by digging in coarse grit and well-rotted compost. The latter will also help in the case of light, sandy soils which lose nutrients quickly and need frequent feeding.

PLANNING

Much has been written about planning and the plants to use. While it is very important that consideration be given to the height and colours of plants, in order to achieve a graduated effect without colour clashes, at the end of the day those incorporated will be very much a personal choice.

A well-planned border will have a selection of plants in varying heights

Successful borders can be achieved by using only certain colours, for example, pink, white and blue, or by restricting the choice to just two colours, for example, white and grey. Borders incorporating the 'hot' colours can also be very effective in the right setting.

Always aim for a border where plants are carefully positioned with regard to height. Check labels for this information or look it up in a catalogue. Most gardeners will go for a mixture, with tall, architectural subjects at the back, graduating down to low-growing perennials at the front. If space is not a problem, island beds are also very attractive; the same principles of gradation apply, but with the taller plants taking centre ground.

Avoid formal arrangements, with plants in rows like soldiers – informal planting is much

Delphiniums can create a striking effect planted at the back of a border

BORDER PLAN 2: SMALL BORDER

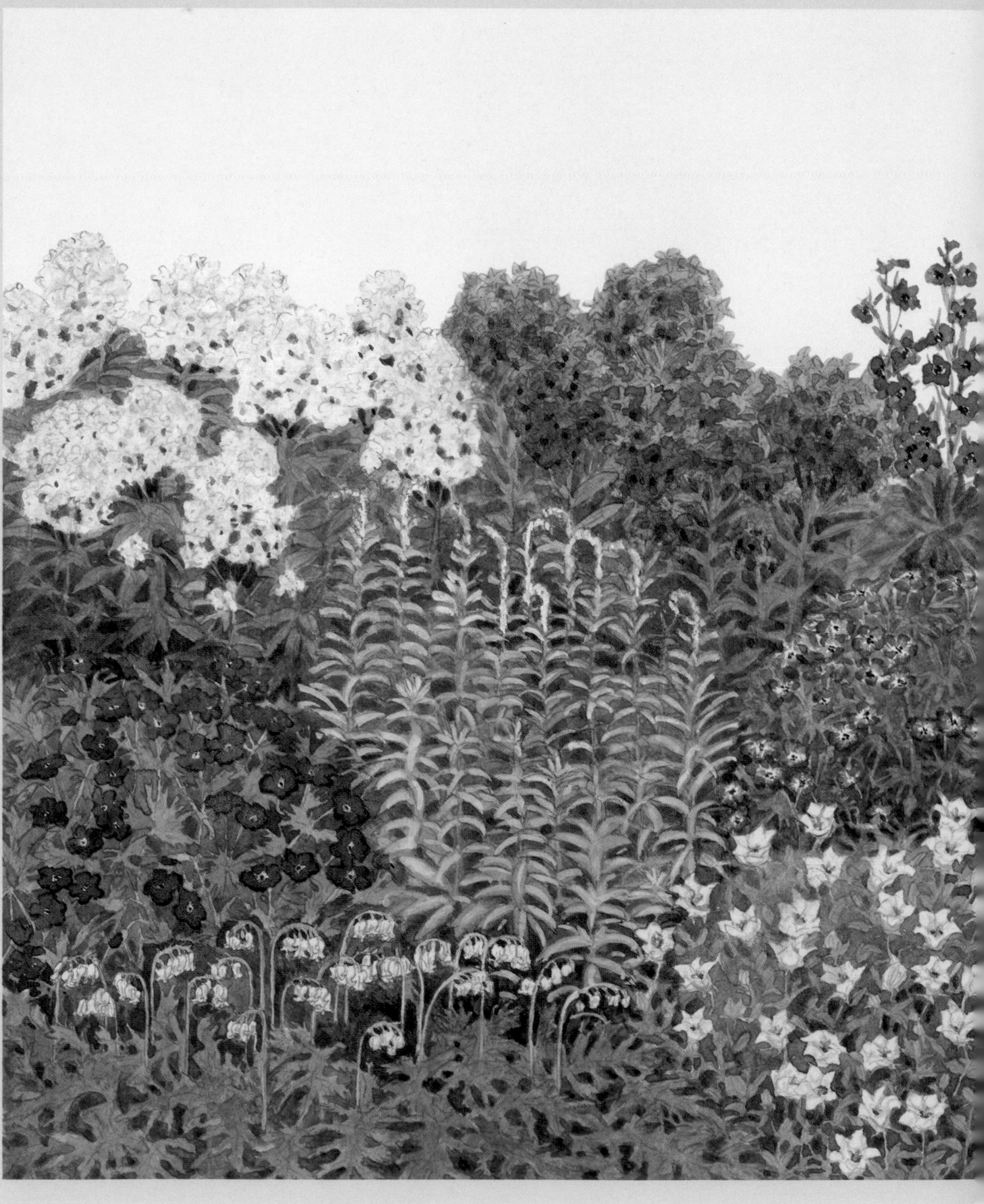

BASED ON BLUE, WHITE AND GREY

KEY TO BORDER PLAN

1 *Dicentra* 'Snowflakes'

2 *Campanula carpatica*

3 *Stachys byzantina*

4 *Geranium* 'Johnson's Blue'

5 *Artemisia* 'Silver Queen'

6 *Geranium* 'Mrs Kendall Clark'

7 *Geranium* 'Kashmir White'

8 *Phlox* 'Fujiyama'

9 *Campanula* 'Prichard's Variety'

10 *Delphinium* 'Peace'

11 *Centranthus ruber albus*

Always choose sturdy plants that are not pot bound and that are free from pests and diseases

A pot-bound plant will have a tight mass of roots which must be gently teased apart before planting

better. This is ideal for annual bedding but not for hardy perennials; these should be planted in small groups of three, five or more, and never in a regimental fashion. Larger plantings are often referred to as drifts. These are splendid for Asiatic primulas and similar types of plants, providing a dramatic display. Remember, once the flowering is over, all that remains to look at, in most cases, is foliage.

PLANTING

Today, most plants are sold container-grown. Purchase the best plants you can find. Look for vigorous, healthy specimens, not necessarily the largest as these may be pot bound and take time to establish; young, vigorous stock will get away quickly. If you do have a pot-bound plant, tease apart the

PLANTING CONTAINER-GROWN PERENNIALS

1 Gently remove the plant from its container, being careful not to damage the roots

2 Dig a hole large enough to accommodate the entire root system

3 Spread and tease out the roots as you position the plant in the hole

4 Backfill to adjust the depth of planting, then firm and water in the plant

Paeonies don't like to be moved once they have settled into their planting place

mass of tightly packed roots before planting. Avoid any plants which show signs of disease or attack by pests (see Chapter 5).

Ideally, container-grown plants should be planted in the spring: they will get away quickly as the days lengthen and the soil warms up. Early-flowering subjects are best set out in the autumn. This will give them time to become established, and they will probably flower in the spring or early summer.

Container-grown plants are usually in soil-less composts, which can be very difficult to re-wet should they dry out – always ensure that they are well watered before planting and that they have sufficient moisture available until well established. This is especially important in hot, dry spells and when new

Before planting, lay out the plants in their pots to get an idea of how the finished arrangement will look. Use sand to mark the area the plants will fill

stock is planted out in the spring, as windy conditions and dry spells can occur at this time. If necessary, stand the plant in 76–102mm/3–4in of water and let this soak into the compost before leaving it to drain. Carefully remove the plant from its container and dig a hole large enough to accommodate the entire root system. If possible, spread out the roots as you position the plant, setting the crown at soil level, then back fill, firm and water in the plant.

When planting a new border it is a good idea to set out the plants still in their containers: this will give you an idea of what the arrangement will look like, and the chance to make any changes should you wish to. Avoid overcrowding: this will result in weak growth and will also increase the possibility of attack by fungal diseases.

Most plant labels now give details of height and spread – read and keep this information, unless you are familiar with a particular subject, as it is very useful. There are some perennials, paeonies being one example, which strongly resent root disturbance, as do other plants with long tap roots. Ensure that you get these in the right position; if you do have to move one later, dig round the plant to retain as much rootball as possible.

A large number of hardy perennials only start into growth in the spring, which can result in a border with very little interest through the winter. There are a few things that can be done to improve this problem.

Many gardeners today favour using perennial plants in a border which also contains shrubs, bulbs and possibly annuals. Shrubs, preferably those which are winter- or

Penstemon 'Sour Grapes' with kniphofias in the background; the tall varieties of kniphofia are superb architectural plants in the right setting

spring-flowering, can be added at the back. Mahonia and some of the viburnums are a good choice. Spring-flowering bulbs will make a fine show early in the year if planted in groups. Their foliage, which remains for several weeks after flowering, should never be cut down or removed as it builds up the bulb for the next season. In most cases it will have died back by early summer, before the perennials really come into their own.

3

PROPAGATION

THERE are several ways of increasing hardy perennials. The method most widely used is division, but this is not applicable to all plants; others are raised from seed, or increased by stem, basal or root cuttings.

Of the equipment needed, a greenhouse is one of the most important items for raising seed and cuttings, although small amounts of seed can be raised on a window sill. The other items required are seed trays, labels, a small dibber, compost and rooting compound. To enable cuttings to root successfully a high humidity is required, and for this a propagator is beneficial. An unheated propagator, which consists of a plastic dome fitted over a seed tray, is sufficient, and available at many garden centres. However, if you are raising a number of plants from seed or cuttings, it may be worthwhile investing in an electric propagator, preferably one with a thermostat: this enables you to have more control, irrespective of the temperature in the greenhouse.

SEED RAISING

Numerous hardy perennials are included in the catalogues of the leading seedsmen. Raising plants by this method enables a considerable number to be produced for a relatively small cost, but some variation in the plants can occur.

Seed is not available for hybrids and named varieties (cultivars) as they do not grow true from seed. They are increased by other means, including cuttings and division, depending on the type of plant.

The seeds of a few plants require soaking or a period of exposure to cold in order to germinate. Study the packet; the necessary treatment will be clearly described where either of these is required.

If you wish to increase stock of a particular plant you can, in many cases, save seed. This should be collected just as it ripens. If necessary, tie a paper bag around the stem just before the seed is shed to ensure that you don't lose any. Collected seed should be stored in a light, airy place and sown at the same time as for commercial seeds.

Extra protection

By enabling much greater control over growing conditions, sowing seed under glass, in a greenhouse or garden frame, has many advantages. The extra protection it provides allows many perennials that would normally be vulnerable in adverse weather conditions to be raised satisfactorily – torrential downpours can soon ruin an outdoor seed bed. However, for some plants (which are identified in the Plant Directory), sowing outdoors in a prepared seed bed is the recommended method.

The best time to sow under glass is in early spring. Use a loam-based or soil-less compost. Usually, more consistent results are achieved using the latter, however, this type of compost requires a careful watch: if it dries out it is very difficult to re-wet and young plants may well be damaged in these conditions. In most cases a standard seed tray is all that is required, but if you are sowing small quantities a plastic half pot, half the depth of a normal pot, is better.

SOWING UNDER GLASS

Fill the container to the rim, ensuring that the compost is spread into the corners and lightly firmed. Level the surface by running a piece of wood along the edges. A very useful piece of equipment for this purpose can be made by attaching a handle to a flat piece of wood, rectangular for trays and round for pots.

Before sowing, water the compost using a fine-rosed watering can and allow to drain. Always sow seed thinly.

Examine the seed. In most cases it can be scattered thinly over the entire surface. To do this, open the packet carefully at one end and gently shake out the seeds to give a good coverage. Fine seed can be mixed with dry silver sand and the mixture sown evenly.

Larger seeds are easiest as they can be spaced by hand on the surface.

Most seeds require a very fine layer of compost to be sprinkled over them. An old kitchen sieve is ideal for this as it gives an even covering. Seeds should never be buried too deeply. As a general rule, stop sprinkling just as the seed disappears. Fine seeds should not be covered at all. Packets these days usually give useful information on sowing and germinating – it is advisable to read these instructions carefully. Seed varieties vary considerably in the length of time they take to germinate; again, approximate times are normally given on the packet.

Having sown the seed, cover the tray with clingfilm or a sheet of glass to keep the temperature even and the humidity high. Place newspaper or brown paper over the top. Any paper and glass should be removed as soon as germination takes place. Some plants require light to germinate, and this will be marked on the packets. In this case, just leave the tray or pot with the clingfilm or glass covering, so that it is open to the light in the greenhouse or frame.

When the seedlings are large enough to handle, prick out into seed trays, holding the leaves carefully and not the stems. Space out into rows and grow on. Alternatively, prick out into 7cm/3in pots. Whether they are in trays or pots, water with a fine-rosed can.

If large enough, the young plants can be planted into their permanent positions in the autumn or overwintered in a garden frame and set into their flowering positions in the spring.

SOWING UNDER GLASS

1 Fill the container with compost, spread it into the corners and level the surface

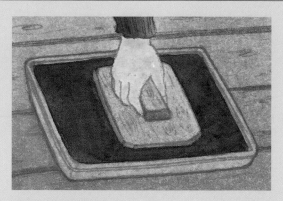

2 Lightly firm the compost

3 Water the compost using a fine-rosed watering can

4a Scatter small seeds thinly over the surface

4b Space larger seeds by hand

5 Sieve a fine layer of compost over the seeds

6   Cover the tray securely with clingfilm or with a sheet of glass

7   Where the seeds do not require light to germinate, place newspaper or brown paper over the glass

8   When large enough to handle, prick the seedlings out into seed trays

9   When the young plants have developed adequately, plant them out into their permanent positions

Sowing outside

The seed of many hardy plants can be sown into a prepared bed in the spring or early summer. Sow in a shallow drill (a furrow), which can be drawn out using a stick. This procedure will make weeding and thinning much easier than if they were sown just by scattering, as the resulting plants will grow in a more orderly fashion.

As with those sown under glass, prick out when large enough to handle, in this case into a nursery bed. To prepare a nursery bed, mark out an area by digging the soil and breaking down the surface to a fine tilth. Keep the seedlings moist. By the following spring or, in some cases, autumn, the majority will be ready to move into their permanent positions.

DIVISION

The majority of hardy plants can be increased by division; the exceptions are those which produce single crowns or long tap roots. Division is the easiest method of propagation.

Some hardy plants will have produced sizable clumps with many crowns and a mass of fibrous roots when the time comes to divide them. These will require two forks placed back-to-back to prise apart divisions. Work from the centre of the plant until the divisions are of a size suitable to split with a hand fork. Retain the vigorous outer sections and discard any old, woody centre pieces. When you have finished dividing, shake each section as free of old soil as possible.

Hardy plants can be divided in the autumn or spring: the hemerocallis pictured here is making new growth and is ready for division

Other perennials are much easier to divide by hand, but the same principles apply. Simply lift the plants and divide, ensuring that each section has roots, growth buds or shoots and discarding any old, woody centre sections.

Start by dividing in half, then divide again and so on, avoiding the temptation to over-divide unless you wish to raise as many plants as possible, as this will result in few flowers the following summer. Replant the new divisions immediately, at the same depth at which they were growing. If you are planting in the same place, rejuvenate the soil first with well-rotted compost or alternatively, with a balanced general fertilizer.

Most hardy perennials can be divided in the autumn, when dormant, or in the spring when they are just starting into growth, never in the height of summer. In cold districts the latter is the best time. Ideally, early-flowering

DIVIDING PLANTS WITH FORKS

Use two forks placed back-to-back to divide perennials with fibrous roots

DIVIDING PLANTS BY HAND

Lift the plant and divide into sections by gently teasing apart the roots

subjects should be divided immediately after flowering. This also applies to tall bearded iris. Michaelmas daisies are best split every two years. In all cases, ensure that the divisions are not short of water, especially in the spring: this will help them to establish quickly.

Remember that division should be used not just to raise new stock but also to keep plants from becoming overcrowded and losing their vigour. As a general rule, divide every three to four years, but as with all rules there are exceptions, in this case subjects which resent disturbance, of which paeonies are a prime example (see individual entries in the Plant Directory). Leave these to increase steadily – they will not lose vigour. Lift and divide only if you require new plants.

DIVIDING RHIZOMATOUS PLANTS

1 Lift the plant gently, being careful around the roots, shake off the soil and pull the rhizomes into separate, manageable pieces

2 Cut off the newer rhizomes and trim

3 Dust the cut surfaces with fungicide and trim the longer roots

4 Plant the rhizomes 12–15cm/5–6in apart

Michaelmas daisies are best divided every two years to keep them healthy

STEM TIP CUTTINGS

Another widely used method of increasing plants is by softwood cuttings. Plants propagated in this way are usually those which grow from a single crown or that do not have suitable foliage for division. Select vigorous, non-flowering shoots and collect them in the morning so that they are fresh. The best time for taking cuttings is during late spring/early summer. They should never be exposed for long as they will quickly lose moisture. Once foliage becomes limp, moisture is not easily recovered, so any loss could result in failure.

Cuttings must be prepared before potting. To do this, trim them below a leaf joint, making a straight cut with a sharp knife, remove the bottom leaves, then dip the base of each cutting in a hormone rooting powder and lightly tap off the surplus. They are now ready for immediate insertion in an equal peat/sand mixture. Place them around the edge of a pot, close to each other but not touching. Finally, firm this mixture lightly around the stem of each cutting.

Cuttings require a constant damp, warm atmosphere and light, so should be placed in a propagator as soon as possible. If your propagator is unheated and you have only a small number of cuttings, place the pot in a polythene bag and seal this before setting the pot in the propagator. As soon as the cuttings have taken root, remove them. They should now be potted up individually into small pots and grown on until ready for planting out – when they are well rooted and making new growth – either in the autumn or, held over in a garden frame, the following spring.

STEM TIP CUTTINGS

1 Take cuttings from shoots that are vigorous and non-flowering

2 Trim the cutting below a leaf joint, remove the bottom leaves, then dip the end in hormone rooting powder

3 Insert the prepared cuttings around the edge of a pot, close but not touching

4 If your propagator is not heated, seal the pot in a plastic bag before placing it inside

BASAL STEM CUTTINGS

This is another propagation method used with many hardy plants (those with hollow or pithy stems), delphiniums and heleniums being two. Basal stem cuttings should be taken in early spring. Select strong, vigorous young shoots of around 6cm/2½in in length and pull carefully from the plant, as close as possible to the crown (the base of the plant). Little is required in the way of preparing a cutting for propagation, except possibly to remove a few of the lower leaves. Follow a similar pattern to stem cuttings with regard to rooting, growing on and planting out.

ROOT CUTTINGS

Thick roots

This method is used with some hardy perennials, prime examples being acanthus, echinacea, phlox and the well-known oriental poppies. It is generally used for plants with fairly thick, fleshy roots. It is a reliable method, even though it may sound complicated. Cuttings should be taken when the plant is dormant. Choose a mild day when the ground is not frozen to lift the parent plant. Wash the soil from its roots in a bucket of water, take those roots required and return the plant to its original position in the border. The cuttings taken should be selected from the thickest sections, and be around 5–10cm/2–4in. Taking a small number of cuttings will not cause any damage; the original plant will grow away happily in the spring as usual and the selected roots can be prepared as cuttings. There is no need to use rooting powder with root cuttings.

It is important to know which is the top of the cutting. Lay the root out and make a straight cut across the top and an angled one across the bottom so that you can identify each end. You will now know which way to insert the cuttings – bottom, angled end first.

BASAL STEM CUTTINGS

1 Pull the cuttings carefully from the crown

2 Remove the lower leaves

3 Prepare and pot the cuttings as for stem tip cuttings

THICK ROOT CUTTINGS

1 Having lifted the dormant plant and washed off the soil, take cuttings from the thickest sections of the roots

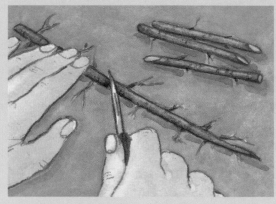

2 Make a straight cut across the top and an angled cut across the bottom of each cutting

Fill the pot with an equal peat/sand mixture, flatten the surface, and simply push the cuttings into the compost so that the top, straight end is level with the surface.

Thin roots

Phlox are also increased by root cuttings, but the cuttings will be thinner. For phlox and other thin-rooted plants of a similar type a

THIN ROOT CUTTINGS

1 Having lifted the dormant plant and washed off the soil, take cuttings from the thickest sections of the roots

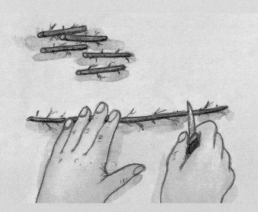

2 Trim the cuttings to around 8–12cm/3–5in, cutting straight across at both ends

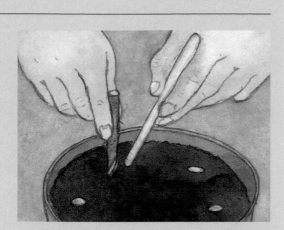

3 Push the cuttings, angled end first, into a pot of equal peat/sand mix so that the straight end is level with the surface

Phlox can be propagated by root cuttings, and as these will not transmit eelworm if present, such cuttings provide pest-free stock

slightly different method is used. Because the cuttings are thinner, they need to be longer – around 8–12cm/3–5in – in order to have a large enough food storing capacity to support the developing cuttings. There is no need to cut straight and angled ends, as the cuttings will not be inserted in a potting mix. Prepare a seed tray with compost, lay the cuttings horizontally, in rows 2.5cm/1in apart, and cover them with a thin layer of compost. Place in a greenhouse or frame and keep moist. Growth will start in the spring. The cuttings should not be left any longer than necessary in the tray, which contains no plant food, but do not be tempted to pot the cuttings individually until new, fibrous roots have been produced. Once they have been, pot individually and grow on. The young plants can be placed in their flowering positions the following spring.

3 Lay the cuttings horizontally, evenly spaced, in a tray filled with compost, cover thinly with compost and place in a greenhouse

4

MAINTENANCE THROUGH THE YEAR

A S WITH so many other things, regular maintenance is all important if hardy perennials are to be kept at their best. Nothing spoils a border more than weeds choking it or plants being blown about during summer storms due to lack of support. Heavy rain and wind combined can knock down many plants which, although they may be tied up immediately when seen, are never the same; once-sturdy stems will have grown towards the light, never to straighten again.

Many perennials have a longer flowering period if they are regularly deadheaded. Failure to do this results in plants turning their attention to producing seed. Even a short time each week spent working on the border pays dividends and makes the job a lot easier.

THE WINTER MONTHS

While inclement weather often restricts working outdoors at this time, opportunities provided by reasonable conditions should not be missed, as winter is an important time in the garden. Firstly, tidy up and remove old leaves and debris which may harbour pests. Some dead stems and foliage can be left until early spring: these help to attract winter insects which, together with the overwintering seed heads themselves, can provide food for birds and small mammals. Cutting back should be done before new growth starts however, as trying to remove old stems after this can be difficult and may cause damage to new shoots. Cut back with a sharp knife to within 5cm/2in of the ground. Some plants are attractive at this time of the year, especially the old stems and flower heads of many grasses, astilbes and eryngiums among them.

In some cold districts, a winter mulch of bracken, straw or leaves will protect the crowns of certain plants from frost damage in severe weather. Any which require this will be mentioned in the individual plant sections. Simply scatter the mulch, to a depth of at least

If the soil is damp, work from a plank of wood. This will spread the load and avoid compacting the soil

15cm/6in, over the crown. Check from time to time that it has not been blown away or moved by high winds.

Never work on very wet or soft soil as this causes compaction and can seriously affect the structure of the soil. If you must complete jobs where the soil is in this condition, use planks to work from.

Remove any weeds and debris that has been blown onto the border during the winter. Weeds with long tap roots should be dug out, taking care not to disturb nearby plants. When this work is finished it is time to apply a top dressing of organic material – well-rotted manure or compost. On clay soils this will improve the aeration and drainage and on light soils, the ability to retain moisture and nutrients. The top dressing should be lightly forked in around the plants.

Fertilizers

There are many organic and inorganic fertilizers on the market and the timing and method of application for each may vary; always follow the manufacturer's instructions.

CUTTING BACK

Cut back the dead stems and foliage to within 5cm/2in of the ground, before any new growth starts

TRANSPLANTING SEEDLINGS

Lift self-sown seedlings gently, being careful not to disturb the root ball, then transfer to a temporary or permanent site, firm in and water thoroughly

EARLY SUMMER WORK

Weeding

This is one of the least appealing but most important jobs. Nothing can spoil a well planned and stocked border more than being choked with weeds. Left they will seed and quickly increase. Careful hoeing can be done when the plants are well spaced, though this does, of course, lead to the possibility of accidentally chopping off new growth. Some perennials are shallow-rooting and can be damaged. Working on the border with a light fork or hand weeding with a trowel are other possibilities. Remove all weeds completely. Chopping only the top growth soon results in a mass of new shoots – it is better to weed a small section thoroughly, returning on another occasion to complete the border, rather than do a rush job.

Some perennials may well self-seed. Keep a careful eye out – young plants can be lifted and planted elsewhere or given to friends.

Applying a mulch

This has a number of advantages, keeping the soil cool in hot weather, helping to retain moisture, and preventing weeds from germinating. It also provides a good visual background for the plants themselves. One of the best mulches is bark. Widely available from garden centres and easily applied, it is clean to use, sterile and will not introduce weed seeds. Another excellent mulch is spent mushroom compost. This can sometimes be more difficult to obtain, and it contains a certain amount of chalk to keep it sweet, which can present problems with lime-hating plants. Other materials that can be used for mulch are straw and grass cuttings, but as both of these are slow to break down and look unsightly, they should only be used at the back of the border. For many years peat was recommended; however, apart from its

Sprinkling a light dressing of general fertilizer around the plants in spring is beneficial. Always take care to avoid sprinkling any on the foliage as this can be burnt by chemicals. Lightly rake in the fertilizer.

Liquid fertilizers should be applied from late spring, up to the plant's producing buds and being in flower. They should usually be applied every fortnight during this time; as always, use as directed.

Slow-release fertilizers are a good choice but avoid any which are too high in nitrogen: while this will lead to lush growth, it will also result in less flowers.

Bonemeal is ideal, as are any of the proprietary slow-release preparations. Again, these should be lightly raked in. Unlike top dressing, these preparations do not improve the structure of the soil in any way. Always take care not to overfeed.

A well watered pulmonaria; these plants will soon droop when they haven't got enough water

permanent positions, especially in hot, dry weather, until well established. Some perennials, pulmonarias being a good example, will soon show they are dry at the roots by flagging; in such circumstances, soak the soil thoroughly.

Deadheading

There are a number of reasons to keep this important job ongoing, the most obvious being appearance – dead flower spikes will certainly spoil the look of a neat, colourful border. More importantly, however, if deadheading is carried out, the plant's energy is channelled into producing more flowers, in some cases a second flush later in the season. If left to their own devices, many will seed

removal destroying wetlands, it has several disadvantages, drying out quickly, blowing away in windy weather and, most important of all, breaking down very quickly and thus failing to do the job for which it was applied.

Watering

As already mentioned, top dressing and mulching both help to preserve moisture and so, reduce the need to water. Whenever watering is required, always give the ground a good soaking, ideally in the early morning or evening: light applications result in plant roots coming near to the surface rather than searching for moisture well down in the soil.

Avoid wetting foliage as in hot, dry weather this can result in unsightly scorching. New plants should always be watered before planting and be kept watered once in their

DEADHEADING

Deadheading will improve the appearance of a plant and prolong flowering; as the flowers begin to fade, remove the spent flower head

PROVIDING SUPPORT

Single stakes are used to support single-stemmed plants; tie the stem to the support loosely with a length of twine

For larger, clump-forming plants, link stakes, which can be raised as the plant grows, should be used to provide support

For smaller clump-forming plants, ring stakes are more suitable than link stakes. As with link stakes, these can be raised to accommodate extra height as the plant grows

Plants with a tendency to droop need the extra support provided by a ring of canes – encircle the clump with canes and loop twine around and between the canes and stems

themselves, with seedlings appearing all over the border. While these are useful as a source of new stock, they can be a nuisance. If you intend to save the seed of a particular plant, leave just a small number of stems; this is usually sufficient.

Among the most popular hardy perennials are the daylilies, hemerocallis to give them their botanical name. As their common name indicates, each individual flower lasts for just one day. If time permits, regular removal of dead flowers greatly improves their appearance. Many gardeners will find this impossible due to other demands on their time; this is not a problem as the dead flowers do eventually fall off.

Providing support

Heavy summer storms and wind can quickly spoil an attractive border – once plants have been blown down they will never look the same again. Preventative measures, especially with susceptible plants, should be taken early. Supports will not show as the foliage grows up around them. There are a number of methods of providing support. The simplest is to use peasticks, which are simply twiggy sticks cut from shrubs and hedgerows. Ideally these should be collected together during the winter. Several sticks surrounding a large clump is usually enough to prevent damage. Some tall-growing plants are best supported by tying individual bamboo canes to each flower spike with soft garden string.

Various types of commercial supports are available from most garden centres and by mail order from specialist firms. There are supports available for single plants (single stakes) as well as for clump-forming subjects (ring and link stakes).

Delphiniums are magnificent plants for the back of a border and are best when each flower spike is tied to a bamboo cane

5

PESTS AND DISEASES

WHEREVER possible, ensure your garden does not provide an inviting home for pests; leaves and dead foliage are particularly attractive to them. Many pests can cause problems, but it is likely that only a few will appear in the average garden. Helpful, illustrated 'Troubleshooters' Guides' are available at many garden centres. These detail different pests and diseases and the appropriate treatments. If you are having problems with a particular pest, visit your local garden centre and consult one of the charts produced by the chemical companies. With these, pests can be easily identified, and the recommended treatment will be given.

PESTS

Slugs and snails

These can be very troublesome as they attack a great variety of plants, especially new spring growth. Some subjects are particularly vulnerable, among them hostas. Slugs and snails can cause considerable damage to plants overnight, damage which remains for the rest of the season.

Suggestions for preventing attack are often seen. One such is to place a ring of grit or ashes around any choice subject. Sadly, these methods are not particularly reliable. If you do have a slug or snail problem, it is more effective to go out after dark with a torch, particularly on a warm, damp evening, and collect them by hand. You will be amazed how many you find. You then have a choice: either destroy them or take them to waste ground well away from your garden. Of course, it is necessary to do this regularly.

There are various proprietary compounds to kill slugs and snails on the market. These are available in both liquid and pellet form, and contain methiocarb or metaldehyde. Always read the label carefully for instructions on their use as these can be dangerous to birds and mammals.

Aphids

The most common aphid is greenfly. Treat affected plants as soon as seen: these pests can build up rapidly. They can distort and weaken new growth, and also transmit viral diseases. Infestation causes the production of a sticky dew; this will eventually become covered with an unpleasant sooty mould which can reduce the levels of light reaching the leaf. There are several products available which can be used to control aphids, ranging from systemic-action insecticides, containing heptenophos, to contact insecticides; primicarb, permethrin and liquid Malathion. Systemic insecticides are absorbed into the plant's sap and thus kill sap-sucking pests. Contact insecticides kill through direct contact with the insect's body. Those listed will also control several other common pests including blackfly and caterpillars. If possible, encourage natural predators to the garden – birds, other insects, spiders, and especially ladybirds.

Vine weevil

Vine weevil has become very troublesome over recent years. The adult beetle attacks leaf edges, but it is what happens below ground that causes the most problems – the white grubs attack the plant's roots. Often the first sign of trouble is when the plant suddenly becomes loose or dies because its roots have been severed. Vine weevil attack numerous plants, but especially primulas. The best method of control is to use a biological pest killer; harmless nematodes watered onto the soil seek out and destroy the grubs. The minimum soil temperature for nematode use is 12°C (54°F). Treatment is recommended twice a year – in the spring and autumn.

Other root pests

After wet winters in particular, leatherjackets can be a problem. These are grey or greyish brown grubs about 2.5cm/1in in length. To treat, sprinkle methiocarb over the ground and rake it lightly in. The larger cutworms, normally around 5cm/2in in length and of a greenish grey or brown, attack both roots and stems. Look out for these when working on the ground and destroy! Treatment consists of using a biological pest killer.

DISEASES

Powdery mildew

Powdery mildew, the symptoms of which are a white, mealy growth on leaves, is often encountered. As this condition is encouraged by overcrowding, always ensure that there is good air circulation around plants. Mildew often strikes during dry weather and when little soil moisture is present. Use a multi-purpose fungicide containing carbendazin to treat. Spray the plant all over as soon as seen and again a few days later. Should the disease reappear, repeat the treatment. This chemical can also be used to treat grey mould.

Viruses

Viral diseases cannot be treated. Symptoms can take many forms, including yellowing, spotting or patches on the foliage, streaking and distortion. Viruses can be transmitted by aphids and other insects and also by tools and fingers. There is no cure; once you are sure that the plants are infected, lift and burn them to prevent the infection spreading.

SAFETY

Always use pesticides and other chemicals carefully, for your own safety and that of animals and other wildlife. Read labels and check that a product is suitable for the plants you wish to treat. Follow the instructions and mix as recommended – never use a stronger solution than quoted. Always store chemicals safely, well away from children and pets.

PRINCIPAL PESTS WHICH MAY AFFECT HARDY PERENNIALS

	Insects and caterpillars	Aphids	Slugs and snails	Vine weevil	Mildew	Stem rot	Viral diseases	Fungal diseases	Crown rot	Eelworm
Acanthus			✗		✗					
Achillea										
Aconitum					✗					
Agapanthus										
Ajuga										
Alchemilla										
Anemone							✗			
Anthemis					✗					
Aquilegia								✗		
Artemisia		✗								
Aruncus	✗									
Aster					✗					
Astilbe										
Astrantia										
Bergenia								✗		
Brunnera										
Caltha					✗					
Campanula			✗					✗		
Coreopsis	✗		✗							
Corydalis										
Delphinium			✗		✗		✗	✗		
Dicentra										
Digitalis									✗	
Doronicum					✗					
Echinacea			✗							
Echinops					✗					
Epilobium	✗									
Epimedium										
Erigeron			✗							
Eryngium	✗									
Eupatorium										
Euphorbia										
Hardy Geraniums			✗	✗	✗					
Geum					✗					
Gypsophila						✗				

	Insects and caterpillars	Aphids	Slugs and snails	Vine weevil	Mildew	Stem rot	Viral diseases	Fungal diseases	Crown rot	Eelworm
Helenium			X							
Helianthus			X		X			X		
Helleborus		X	X					X		
Hemerocallis			X							
Hosta			X	X						
Inula										
Iris							X	X		
Kniphofia								X		
Lamium					X					
Liatris			X							
Liriope			X							
Lupinus		X					X	X		
Lychnis							X			
Lysichiton										
Lysimachia										
Lythrum										
Nepeta					X					
Oenothera					X					
Paeonia								X		
Papaver					X					
Penstemon										
Persicaria										
Phlox			X		X					X
Polemonium					X					
Primula				X			X	X		
Pulmonaria			X		X					
Rheum										
Rudbeckia			X							
Sedum			X	X				X		
Sisyrinchium				X						
Solidago					X					
Stachys					X					
Trillium			X							
Verbascum	X				X					
Zantedeschia							X			

THE PLANT
DIRECTORY

ACANTHUS

Common name: Bear's breeches
Family: Acanthaceae

Acanthus spinosus (AGM); introduced over 300 years ago and commonly known as bear's breeches. An excellent architectural plant for the border

These are handsome, sun-loving border plants of architectural quality, with attractive, deep green, spiny and pointed basal leaves. The stiff, distinctive flower spikes of the two most popular species, *Acanthus mollis* and *spinosus*, both reach 120cm/47in, with overlapping bracts and tubular, mauve, foxglove-like flowers. Although they will grow in lightly shaded areas, they are unlikely to be as free flowering. Once established they are vigorous plants with a running rootstock, so a planting distance of around 90cm/36in should be allowed. Acanthus can be kept in check easily by digging around the plant and removing any pieces of severed rootstock: these will form new plants unless removed. Self-seeding can also be a nuisance but this can, of course, be prevented by cutting off dead flower spikes before they have the chance to set seed.

SPECIES AND VARIETIES

Acanthus spinosus is a native of south east Europe, introduced to Britain in the early 1600s. It flowers in late summer, is easy to grow and widely available from nurserymen and garden centres. It grows to a height of around 120cm/47in.

Acanthus mollis, an Italian species, was introduced before *A. spinosus*. It also grows to around 120cm/47in, and has long, dull green, spiky foliage. There are several varieties including 'Fielding Gold', 'Hollard's Gold' and others that are listed as the Latifolius Group, all with larger foliage. The mauve pink flowers are attractive and produced more sparingly. The flower spikes can be dried and used for winter decoration, though care should be taken when handling due to the sharp prickles.

CULTIVATION

Soil type Deep, well drained, humus-rich soil.

Planting Ideally, acanthus should be planted in the spring. Most are supplied container-grown and can be planted anytime between October and March so long as the soil is in a suitable condition; they should never be planted in very wet or frosty conditions. Once planted they can be left undisturbed to produce sizable clumps.

Maintenance Established plants will benefit from a top dressing of well-rotted compost in the spring, or an application of a suitable slow-release fertilizer, lightly raked in. After flowering, cut the flower stems down to almost ground level. In cold districts new plants should be protected by a mulch of straw or bracken for the first winter.

Propagation This can be by seed, root cuttings or division. Sow in seed boxes and place in a cold frame. Prick out into a sheltered nursery bed when large enough to handle. Grow on for two years before planting into their permanent positions.

Root cuttings should be approximately 8cm/3in in length, taken from December to February, and placed in boxes of sandy soil in a garden frame. When well rooted and making new growth, transfer them to a nursery bed and grow on.

Lift and carefully divide in early spring, retaining strong outer sections but discarding old woody portions. Replant immediately.

Pests and diseases Generally acanthus are trouble free though new growth can be attacked by snails and slugs. In dry weather mildew can be a problem – treat with a suitable fungicide.

ACHILLEA

COMMON NAME: YARROW
FAMILY: ASTERACEAE

Of the considerable number of species in this family, many are suitable for the rock garden while others are splendid, easily grown hardy perennials for the border; it is the latter which concern us here. The flower heads of achillea, which bloom for a long period, can be loose clusters or flat heads comprised of a mass of tiny daisy-like flowers. The yellow, flat-headed varieties are especially useful for drying and for winter decorations.

Achillea filipendulina 'Gold Plate' (AGM); a good form of this very useful, summer-flowering plant

SPECIES AND VARIETIES The achilleas grown in our gardens today are mostly cultivars or hybrids. One of the most spectacular is 'Gold Plate' (AGM) which grows to 1.2m/4ft, with flat heads of deep golden yellow. 'Coronation Gold' (AGM) is another first class variety; it reaches 90cm/36in, with rich golden yellow flower heads in the summer. Another good plant for the border is 'Cerise Queen', with cherry red

Achillea 'Fanal', formerly 'The Beacon'; attractive, fern-like foliage, easy to grow and widely available

flowers in June and July. Many achilleas have been raised in Germany and these are sometimes referred to as 'Galaxy Hybrids'. All have deep green, feathery foliage reaching 60cm/24in in height, making them ideal border plants. They include 'Apple Blossom' (more correctly 'Apfelblüte'), 'Salmon Beauty' (more correctly 'Lachsschönheit'), a light salmon pink, and one of the best known, 'Fanal' (syn. 'The Beacon'), a lovely bright red.

CULTIVATION

Soil type Achilleas are sun lovers which do well in light, well drained, fertile soil.

Planting This can be done in the autumn or spring. If planting in spring, ensure that new plants have sufficient moisture during hot dry spells until well established.

Maintenance Most should not require supporting except in very windy spots. If this is necessary, using pea sticks half the way up the plant should be sufficient. Cutting back after flowering may well produce a further flush of flowers. In the autumn, remove dead foliage and any old stems.

Propagation Carefully lift and divide the roots in early spring, retaining strong outer portions with four or five shoots. Discard old centre sections. Rejuvenate the soil by incorporating well-rotted compost and replant immediately. Division should be done every three years to prevent the plants losing vigour and flowering less; if left longer, the centre of the clumps can die out.

Pests and diseases Achilleas are ideal subjects as they are generally free of pests and diseases.

ACONITUM

COMMON NAMES: MONKSHOOD, HELMET FLOWER, WOLF'S BANE
FAMILY: RANUNCULACEAE

This family of plants includes many hardy, free-flowering perennials, some blooming late in the season. All those mentioned below produce tuberous roots. Aconitum generally, especially the roots, are poisonous. Their distinctive hooded flowers have given rise to the common name monkshood. While they are best in an open, sunny position, provided a plentiful supply of moisture is present, they will also grow well in a lightly shaded spot. Once planted leave undisturbed for four to five years; left longer than this, they will almost certainly have exhausted the nutrients in the soil, leading to smaller plants and less flowers produced.

Aconitum x *cammarum* 'Bicolor'; a distinctive plant with hooded flowers, giving rise to its common name 'monkshood'. Poisonous

SPECIES AND VARIETIES

There are four named varieties which hold the coveted RHS Award of Garden Merit. 'Bressingham Spire' (AGM), its violet blue, hooded flowers held on strong 90cm/36in stems with side spikes, flowers from July through to September; x *cammarum* 'Bicolor' (AGM), as its name suggests, has a distinctive combination of violet blue and white on branching stems; 'Kelmscott' (AGM) is a handsome lavender blue. The final one, 'Spark's Variety' (AGM), is a real old stager, introduced around 1898, which has stood the test of time well. It has impressive dark violet blue flowers. In contrast is another splendid variety, 'Ivorine', a vigorous bushy plant with ivory white flowers on branching stems, from June onwards.

CULTIVATION

Soil type Aconitums enjoy cool, moist, humus-rich soil.

Planting Growth starts early, often in February. Ideally, plant in the autumn, though they can be planted up to March, provided soil conditions are right; never plant when cold, wet or frosty.

Maintenance Some varieties require staking but nothing spoils the display more than bamboo canes sticking out above the foliage. Using pea sticks is much more satisfactory: these will, as the plant grows, become hidden in the foliage, at the same time providing support. Regular deadheading and removal of old stems can often lead to further flowers on some varieties. Tidy up in the autumn – old stems will come away easily in winter but remember that growth starts early.

Propagation As with so many hardy perennials, division is the method of propagation. Lift in autumn or early spring, divide the tubers, select the strongest and replant immediately. If planting in the same spot, do not forget to rejuvenate the soil by adding well-rotted compost and a balanced fertilizer.

Pests and diseases While they are generally trouble free, aconitums are prone to powdery mildew late in the season; if mildew does attack, cut back affected foliage and burn.

AGAPANTHUS

COMMON NAME: AFRICAN LILY
FAMILY: ALLIACEAE

Agapanthus Headbourne Hybrids; a strain with varying shades of blue and widely available

These very colourful plants are native to South Africa. There are several species available, some of which require winter protection. The numerous hybrids are generally regarded as hardier growing in all but the coldest districts. Agapanthus range in height from 45–90cm/ 18–36in and are available with blue or white flowers. The foliage is dark green, in some cases narrow, in others strap-shaped (wide and flat). They may be evergreen or deciduous. Those which retain their foliage are generally not so hardy and are best grown in tubs which can be moved under cover for the winter. It is those with narrow foliage, all deciduous, that are more hardy. With the exception of the south and west of Britain, agapanthus should be grown in a sheltered, sunny border, with winter protection from mid-autumn to early spring in the form of bracken, chipped bark or even coarse sand, especially in the coldest districts. Agapanthus are good cut flowers and the stems can be dried and used for winter decorations.

SPECIES AND VARIETIES One of the most attractive species is *Agapanthus campanulatus* subsp. *patens* (AGM); the stout flower spikes of 1.2m/4ft are held over greyish foliage and have heads of lovely clear light blue flowers. Among the numerous named varieties are the well known and widely available 'Headbourne Hybrids'. These range from deep violet to pale blue, their flowers on strong, 75cm/30in stems. Others to look out for are 'Lilliput', a dwarf, rich blue on 30cm/12in stems, which is ideal for smaller gardens. 'Isis' is another good choice with blue flowers – one of several splendid agapanthus introduced by Bressingham.

With the current wide interest in white flowers, 'Bressingham White' is a good choice, free-flowering, with its flower heads on strong 90cm/36in stems.

CULTIVATION

Soil type Agapanthus are sun lovers and are easily grown given good humus-rich, well drained, moisture-retentive soil. They will not grow in cold, wet conditions.

Planting Plant in the spring with the growing points just below the surface. Once planted leave undisturbed. They can remain in the same spot for several years, building up into a sizable clump with annual feeding. Only when flowering is affected or they are becoming seriously overgrown is it necessary to take action.

Maintenance Always ensure a plentiful supply of moisture during the growing period, especially after planting in hot, dry spells. Remove dead flower spikes rather than leaving them to produce seed – this, in turn, will help to conserve the plant's energy. In the autumn, tidy any dead foliage and old flowering stems.

Propagation The time to increase stock is in the spring, by division. Lift and carefully divide, taking care not to damage the fleshy roots. If possible, replant immediately in a new spot. If you do plant in the same place, rejuvenate the soil by digging in well-rotted compost and a balanced fertilizer. Agapanthus can be grown from seed which usually germinates well, but it does take several years before the plants reach flowering size.

Pests and diseases These elegant plants are generally trouble free.

AJUGA

COMMON NAME: BUGLE
FAMILY: LAMIACEAE

These are good ground cover plants with attractive foliage and, in early summer, short spikes of attractive flowers. There are a number of varieties with colourful leaves which have become very popular in recent years. Moisture loving, they are ideal in an open, sunny position. While they will tolerate light shade, the coloured leaves are likely to turn green and less flowers will be produced.

Ajuga 'Pink Surprise'; there are several varieties of these good ground cover plants with pink flowers

Ajuga reptans 'Braunherz' (AGM); prostrate mats of dark, metallic foliage and spikes of rich blue flowers

SPECIES AND VARIETIES

Unlike the others, *Ajuga pyramidalis* forms a neat clump of foliage – established plants are unlikely to be more than 30cm/12in across and 25cm/10in in height. It is grown mainly for its 15cm/6in spikes of blue flowers with purple bracts, freely produced in May. 'Metallica Crispa' is more vigorous and has lovely purple bronze foliage with an almost metallic sheen. By far the most numerous members of this family in cultivation are varieties of *Ajuga reptans*, a native species which is also found in many other parts of Europe. There are many varieties of this plant with its rich leaf colouring, including 'Braunherz' (AGM), a shiny purple bronze, and 'Burgundy Glow' (AGM), which has handsome maroon and cream foliage and pretty light blue flowers. Both of these grow to around 15cm/6in. 'Catlin's Giant', reaching up to 25cm/10in, is another award holder. It has typical ajuga flowers and is a larger, more vigorous plant generally. 'Multicolor' (syn. 'Rainbow') is also worth looking out for. It is difficult to describe this one, a mixture of bronze, pink and yellow. There are several varieties with pink flowers, which presents a change from the more usual blue. One which is certainly a worthwhile addition is 'Pink Surprise'. I personally would not overlook 'Atropurpurea' (AGM) – its shiny purple leaves are a pleasing sight in any winter's sunshine.

CULTIVATION

Soil type Easy in most fertile, moisture-retentive soils, it will also grow in heavy types. They do not like hot, dry, sandy soil.

Planting This can be done either in the autumn or spring, or at any other time providing the soil is not wet or frozen.

Maintenance There is little to do during the season except deadheading. Ajugas, with the exception of *A. pyramidalis*, spread rapidly so their position should be chosen with care.

Propagation Simply lift and divide, retaining strong outer portions. If you divide in the spring you are unlikely to get flowers in early summer. Early autumn is the best time, giving divisions time to re-establish before winter.

Pests and diseases Just as gardeners like – generally trouble free.

ALCHEMILLA

COMMON NAME: LADY'S MANTLE
FAMILY: ROSACEAE

The member of this family most likely to be seen in our gardens is *Alchemilla mollis*, with its handsome grey green foliage and masses of yellow green, feathery sprays which flower over several weeks from early summer onwards. Ideal for cutting and widely used by flower arrangers. Splendid as this plant unquestionably is, it does have one failing – its self-seeding habit. The seedlings manage to find many different spots, including cracks in paving and among other plants. Weeding out seedlings by hand while they are small or regularly deadheading the plant before it has a chance to set seed will help to prevent this problem; deadheading is the best method of control.

Alchemilla mollis (AGM); masses of yellow green flowers over grey green foliage. Commonly known as lady's mantle, this will grow well in many types of soil

SPECIES AND VARIETIES

Alchemilla mollis (AGM) is widely available. It was first introduced to our gardens in the 1870s. The grey green, downy leaves are attractive in their own right. Rounded and with a serrated edge, they hold raindrops in their centre. Established plants can easily reach 45cm/18in across. Alchemillas have many uses in the garden, being ideal for the border and very attractive at the edge of a pond. Flowering commences in June and goes on for several weeks.

CULTIVATION

Soil type These graceful plants will grow in most fertile, moist garden soils in full sun or shade. One condition they will not tolerate is waterlogged soil.

Planting Plant either in the autumn or spring, in a well drained position.

Maintenance There is little to be done during the growing season except deadheading. In the autumn, cut back old stems and foliage.

Propagation Alchemillas can be propagated by division or by seed. Division can be done in the autumn or spring, whenever soil conditions are suitable. Seed should be sown in March, in pots of John Innes seed compost. When large enough to handle, prick out into pots and grow on, planting into flowering positions in the autumn or spring. Self-sown seedlings can usually be found near established plants; lift, pot, and treat in the same way.

Pests and diseases These are not usually troubled by pests and diseases.

ANEMONE

COMMON NAME: JAPANESE ANEMONES
FAMILY: RANUNCULACEAE

Japanese anemones; useful late-flowering plants with a spreading habit

The Japanese anemones are very useful, long-lived plants. They are indispensable for adding colour to the border in late summer and well into autumn. Once planted, either in full sun or light shade, they can be left undisturbed for years, eventually building up into sizable clumps.

SPECIES AND VARIETIES   The named varieties of anemone available today include some which have stood the test of time well. 'Whirlwind', a semi-double white, was introduced well over 100 years ago and is still widely available. Another old stager is the semi-double pink 'Queen Charlotte', or now more correctly 'Königin Charlotte' (AGM). The pink-flowered varieties are always popular – 'Bressingham Glow', a rich deep pink semi-double, grows to 60cm/24in in height. There are many more splendid varieties available from nurserymen who specialize in hardy perennials.

CULTIVATION

Soil type Most well drained soils, including alkaline.

Planting September or March. Choose the position carefully as they can become invasive when well established.

Maintenance If the plants look like extending beyond their space, dig round every year, taking care to remove any pieces that have broken off, as these will invariably root and form a new plant. Tidy up the site in late autumn.

Propagation These anemones are increased from root cuttings taken between November and January. Insert the cuttings in trays containing an equal peat/sand mix and place in a frame. When new growth has commenced, lift and plant out in nursery rows. Move into their permanent positions in the autumn of the following year. Another method is to cut off a small, rooted section without disturbing the plant and move this to a new position; this should be done in the spring.

Pests and diseases There are a number of viral diseases which can affect these plants – this usually shows as yellowing foliage and stunting. Lift infected plants and destroy.

ANTHEMIS

COMMON NAME: OX-EYE CHAMOMILE
FAMILY: ASTERACEAE

The most widely grown hardy perennial members of this family are hybrids. These are sun loving and easily grown, ideal subjects for a border.

Anthemis 'E. C. Buxton'; a sun lover with masses of lemon yellow daisies in the summer

SPECIES AND VARIETIES   The plants mentioned here are to be found listed under *Anthemis tinctoria*, also known as 'Golden Chamomile'. Those to look out for are 'E. C. Buxton', which has masses of lemon yellow daisies, 'Sauce Hollandaise', a pale yellow variety growing to 45cm/18in, and 'Wargrave Variety', a delightful creamy yellow – all are widely available. There is a white form listed simply as *Anthemis tinctoria* 'Alba'.

CULTIVATION   **Soil type** Most fertile, well drained, ordinary soils.

Planting September or March, in a sunny position.

Maintenance In exposed positions support may be needed; this is best done with twiggy sticks. In the autumn, cut down old growth and tidy up.

Propagation Division in the autumn or spring is the easiest method. Cuttings can be taken in the spring using 5cm/2in basal shoots. Root in an equal mix of peat and sand, place in a garden frame, and when well rooted, transfer to a nursery bed. In the autumn or following spring, plant out into their flowering positions.

Pests and diseases Mildew can be a problem, especially with older plants. Treat with a fungicide.

AQUILEGIA

COMMON NAME: COLUMBINE
FAMILY: RANUNCULACEAE

One plant, a great favourite in cottage gardens, is *Aquilegia vulgaris*, with its short, spurred flowers of several colours – the violet form is the one most commonly seen. Today a much wider choice of these very handsome plants is available, including numerous named varieties and the long-spurred McKana Hybrids.

Aquilegia 'Matthew Stromminger'; free-flowering with masses of rich deep pink flowers

Aquilegias are available in a wide range of colours. They will normally self-seed

SPECIES AND VARIETIES   The common columbine *Aquilegia vulgaris* is generally known as granny's bonnets. It is the named varieties which are widely seen; 'Nora Barlow' (AGM) with its double rose and white flowers, the white 'Nivea' (AGM) and the distinctive golden foliage of 'Granny's Gold' which contrasts well with its purple flowers. The McKana Hybrids, with their distinctive long spurs, have a range of colours.

CULTIVATION   **Soil type** Most humus-rich, well drained soils are suitable. They do best in moisture-retentive soil.

Planting Aquilegias are not long lived, they do self-seed freely although they may well not come true. Planting can be done either in the autumn or spring.

Maintenance Regular deadheading will help to prevent unwanted seedlings. Where any seedlings are present and you wish to transplant them, do so only when they are young as they resent disturbance. Cut back old stems and tidy up in the autumn.

Propagation Sow seed in the spring in trays of John Innes No. 1 compost and place in a garden frame. When large enough to handle, prick out into 7cm/3in pots. Plant into their flowering positions in the autumn.

Pests and diseases There are a number of fungal diseases which can attack aquilegias – treat with a fungicide as soon as seen. If the attack is after flowering, the foliage should be cut down and burnt.

ARTEMISIA

COMMON NAME: WORMWOOD
FAMILY: ASTERACEAE

Artemisia 'Silver Queen' (AGM); vigorous, with mats of silver foliage and stems, makes a good background for many plants

Artemisia schmidtiana 'Nana' (AGM); low-growing, with mats of silver foliage, suitable for placement at the front of a border

These plants are generally grown for their attractive, often silvery, toothed or finely cut foliage which is a perfect background for many other perennials. They are easily grown in light, well drained soils.

SPECIES AND VARIETIES

There are numerous species available, but as with so many hardy plants, it is the named varieties which are the most popular and widely grown. Several have been awarded the RHS Award of Garden Merit. These include the vigorous 'Silver Queen' with its silvery foliage growing to 80cm/32in in height, 'Lambrook Silver', slightly taller, with glossy silvery foliage, and the popular hybrid 'Powis Castle', a shrubby plant with finely cut foliage.

CULTIVATION

Soil type Artemisias are sun lovers which grow well in light, well drained soils. As with most rules there are exceptions, in this case *Artemisia lactiflora*, which prefers a heavier, moisture-retentive soil.

Planting This is best done in the spring: as the soil warms up the plants will get away quicker. Ensure that they have sufficient moisture until well established. Choose an open, sunny spot; the hardy perennials will tolerate lightly shaded areas.

Maintenance The perennials should be cut back almost to ground level in the autumn. The shrubby types, which include 'Powis Castle', should be pruned in the spring to keep the plant in good shape. Always check for signs of new growth appearing before carrying out this work.

Propagation The perennials can be lifted and divided in the spring, then replanted immediately. The shrubby types are increased by semi-ripe cuttings, taken with a heel during August. Trim and place the cuttings in a pot containing an equal peat and sand mixture and place in a garden frame. The following spring, pot up individually into 7cm/3in pots, grow on and plant out in the autumn or spring.

Pests and diseases Young growth can be attacked by aphids in the spring; spray with insecticide as soon as seen.

ARUNCUS

COMMON NAME: GOAT'S BEARD
FAMILY: ROSACEAE

These are graceful, moisture loving, hardy herbaceous perennials, generally more suited to larger gardens. The huge, creamy-white plumes are very spectacular either in a border or at the side of a garden pool.

SPECIES AND VARIETIES   *Aruncus dioicus* is a sizable plant with broad, fern-like foliage, surmounted in the summer with strong stems of 1.2m/4ft carrying its eye-catching plumes. The variety 'Kneifii' (AGM) is more in keeping with smaller gardens, reaching just 60cm/24in in height. Although much smaller, it is every bit as desirable, with its finely divided foliage.

Aruncus dioicus (syn. *A. sylvester*); widely known as goat's beard, does best in moist conditions

CULTIVATION

Soil type Most humus-rich soils. Aruncus are happy in a sunny spot provided it does not dry out – they are moisture lovers – or in light shade.

Planting This can be either in the autumn or spring. Prepare the ground well by digging over and incorporating humus.

Maintenance Aruncus do not require supporting. They are self-seeders but cutting down as soon as flowering finishes will prevent this. In the autumn, cut back to ground level and tidy up.

Propagation This is by lifting and dividing in the autumn. Select strong outer portions and replant immediately. If replanting in the same spot, incorporate plenty of well-rotted compost.

Pests and diseases The foliage of aruncus can be reduced to little more than a skeleton by the larvae of sawfly. Immediately an attack is seen, spray with a contact insecticide.

ASTER

COMMON NAME: MICHAELMAS DAISY
FAMILY: ASTERACEAE

Aster amellus 'Vanity'; this is a great favourite with butterflies

Mention aster and most gardeners will think of two types; those grown as annuals and the best-known of all, the Michaelmas daisies, though these two by no means comprise all within this large group of plants. It is the later-flowering kinds which concern us here, principal among them the very colourful Michaelmas daisies which, strictly, refers to *Aster novi-belgii*. Looking through the vast number of varieties which come within this group, it soon becomes apparent that several carry the name 'Ballard'. These were raised many years ago by Ernest Ballard of Colwall, Malvern, in England, and include one which is still as popular today – the mauve blue 'Ada Ballard', which flowers on 90cm/36in stems. One of the finest reds is 'Beechwood Supreme', which grows to the same height. Another good red, ideal for the middle of the border, is 'Beechwood Charm'.

Aster amellus 'Sonia'; this variety is one of the best deep pinks of this popular, autumn-flowering plant

SPECIES AND VARIETIES   There is a whole host of these asters with flowers of varying shades of blue. A very deep Oxford blue with semi-double flowers is 'Blue Rocket', a taller variety growing to 1.2m/4ft. 'Blue Patrol' is also very useful, producing its violet blue, semi-double flowers later in the season. The pink semi-double, 'Elizabeth Hutton', is another good choice, as is the white, green-centred, semi-double 'Arctic'. Michaelmas daisies are unsurpassable for autumn colour in the border – by choosing carefully, it is possible to have them in flower from early September until well into November. The *novae-angliae* varieties, often referred to as 'New England' asters, are splendid plants for the back of the border: tall and majestic, they provide a splendid autumn display.

Though with nowhere near so many varieties, one not to overlook is 'Andenken an Alma Potschke' (AGM), a lovely salmon pink and one of the most popular, reaching 1.2m/4ft in height. Another well worth including in the border is 'Herbstschnee', a white with yellow centre, sometimes listed as 'Autumn Snow'.

An up-and-coming new introduction is 'Christopher Harbutt'. This has rich purple flowers with a prominent yellow centre and, like so many, a great attraction for butterflies. One very important point to remember with this group is their resistance to mildew.

Michaelmas daisies are not all tall. 'Professor Anton Kippenburg' is an eye-catching bright blue reaching just 30cm/12in – very attractive when planted alongside the white-flowered 'Kristina'. There are many other fine asters, including *A. ericoides* 'Pink Cloud' (AGM), with masses of small, starry flowers on 85cm/34in stems, *A. cordifolius* 'Silver Spray', with a profusion of silvery

Aster x *frikartii* 'Mönch' (AGM); raised in Switzerland many years ago, one of three named after famous mountains in the Jungfrau range

blue, star-shaped flowers, and *A.* x *frikartii* 'Mönch' (AGM). 'Mönch' is one of three raised in Switzerland in the 1920s and named after famous mountains in the Jungfrau group, the other two being 'Eiger' and 'Jungfrau'. The best, in my opinion, is 'Mönch', which has lavender blue flowers from midsummer on into October.

CULTIVATION

Soil type Most fertile garden soils, preferably those which do not become too dry.

Planting This can be done in either the spring or autumn. Choose an open position with good air circulation.

Maintenance Regular division, every two or three years, will keep them vigorous; select strong outer portions for replanting, discard old centre woody sections. Some of the taller varieties may need supporting with twiggy sticks. Cut down old stems and tidy up in late autumn.

Propagation Division is an easy method of increasing stock. It is also possible to use single-rooted shoots, but it will take longer, following this method, for sizable plants to build up.

Pests and diseases Unfortunately, Michaelmas daisies of the *novi-belgii* group are prone to mildew; regular spraying with fungicide is beneficial. Aster wilt can also be a problem; the best solution for this condition is to burn any infected plants.

ASTILBE

COMMON NAME: FALSE GOAT'S BEARD
FAMILY: SAXIFRAGACEAE

One thing to remember with astilbes is to plant them in moist soil, either in full sun or light shade. They are splendid plants for the side of a pool and will tolerate quite wet conditions.

Astilbe 'Irrlicht'; one of several white varieties available

SPECIES AND VARIETIES

The most popular members of this family are those grouped under *Astilbe* x *arendsii*, a hybrid which was first introduced in the early 1900s. Since then many named varieties have appeared in a range of colours, most of which are still available. Among these is 'Fanal' (AGM), which flowers early with 60cm/24in spikes of dark crimson red. Another good choice is 'Fire', or more correctly 'Feur', later flowering with 90cm/36in feathery spikes of eye-catching coral red. The lovely lilac pink, early flowering 'Amethyst' was first introduced as far back as 1920 and is still among the most popular. Look out also for the pure white 'Irrlicht'.

All of those mentioned are varieties of *Astilbe* x *arendsii*, by no means all that are available. Among the numerous hybrids are the white 'Deutschland', flame red 'Montgomery' and rich pink 'Rheinland' (AGM), which is an old favourite. There are a great many more, all splendid plants. An excellent subject for the edge of a pool is the low-growing *Astilbe chinensis* var. *pumila* (AGM). Flowering from August onwards, the mauve pink flower spikes appear over a dense mat of foliage.

CULTIVATION

Soil type Astilbes are moisture lovers; they are happy in full sun provided they are not short of moisture. If they do become short, the foliage will droop, and if not rectified quickly, it will soon turn brown. Most humus-rich soils are suitable. They are excellent plants for a lightly shaded spot and look particularly effective in small groups.

Planting This can be done in the autumn or spring; in spring, care should be taken to ensure they do not suffer from lack of moisture.

Maintenance You can remove the dead flower spikes during the season or leave them for winter decoration – the rusty brown seed heads look particularly effective; remove just before growth commences in the spring. The roots of astilbes are near the surface, so weed by hand rather than using tools, which will damage the plant. In late winter apply a mulch of well-rotted compost: this will feed the plant and at the same time help to suppress weed growth. Every three years, lift and divide the plants or they will become congested, causing them to lose vitality and flower less. In hot, dry weather, always keep well watered.

Propagation Carefully lift and divide either in the autumn or early spring. Retain strong outer portions and discard any old, woody centre growth. Replant, ideally in a fresh spot or having first rejuvenated the soil by incorporating plenty of well-rotted compost.

Pests and diseases Astilbes are usually trouble free.

Astilbe 'Rheinland' (AGM); a moisture lover with large, feathery, deep pink flower heads

ASTRANTIA

COMMON NAME: MASTERWORT
FAMILY: APIACEAE

The flowers of this popular herbaceous perennial have attractive blooms, albeit curiously shaped, comprising a dome of tiny florets surrounded by narrow, parchment-like bracts which give them a star-like appearance.

Astrantia 'Claret'; a clump-forming plant with interesting and unusual flowers

SPECIES AND VARIETIES   The most widely available species is *Astrantia major*, with starry, greenish white flowers on 60cm/24in stems. There are a number of splendid named varieties, including 'Hadspen Blood' and 'Ruby Wedding', both with deep red flowers, 'Claret', a deep, rich pink and 'Shaggy' with extra-large bracts. 'Sunningdale Variegated' is very effective early in the season – its leaves with white streaks fade when the flowers appear.

CULTIVATION   **Soil type** Astrantias are happy in most ordinary garden soils.

Planting This can be done either in the autumn or spring, ideally in a moist, partially shaded spot. They will grow successfully in full sun, provided sufficient moisture is present.

Maintenance Astrantias do not normally require support unless in an exposed position. Deadhead regularly to prevent self-seeding. In the autumn, cut back dead foliage and tidy the site.

Propagation Lift and divide either in the autumn or spring. Discard old, woody portions and replant immediately, rejuvenating the soil beforehand. Astrantia can also be grown from seed; sow in boxes of John Innes seed compost in the autumn and place in a cold frame. Prick out when large enough to handle and grow on. Plant into their flowering positions the following spring.

Pests and diseases Generally trouble free plants.

BERGENIA

COMMON NAME: ELEPHANT'S EARS
FAMILY: SAXIFRAGACEAE

Bergenia 'Silberlicht' (AGM); these plants, because of their tough leathery leaves, are known by the common name elephant's ears

These plants, with their leathery leaves, are among the first hardy perennials to flower. Often the buds can be seen in late winter awaiting the right time to grow away. Some varieties take on attractive autumn tints while others are particularly useful, having rich mahogany red foliage throughout the winter, turning green in the spring. It is the sizable, rounded, tough leaves of these plants that has resulted in the common name elephant's ears. Bergenias are good ground cover plants which can be left undisturbed until they eventually become overcrowded. The flower stems are strong and are topped with a head of white, pink, magenta and crimson flowers.

SPECIES AND VARIETIES While the species are available, those which are popular are hybrids. There is an excellent selection from which to choose, many raised in Germany, several others originating from Bressingham, in Norfolk. One of the earliest to flower is *Bergenia* x *schmidtii* (AGM), with shiny foliage and pink flowers on 30cm/12in stems. An old favourite is 'Ballawley' (AGM). Raised in Ireland over 50 years ago, it has lovely bright crimson flowers. Of those raised in England, 'Bressingham White' (AGM) is a good choice, its white flower heads on 30cm/12in stems held well clear of the foliage. Look out also for the aptly named 'Bressingham Salmon'. Others which will certainly not disappoint are 'Abendglut' (Evening Glow), with magenta/crimson flowers and maroon winter foliage, 'Morgenrote' (Morning Blush) (AGM), a deep, carmine pink, and 'Silberlicht' (Silver light) (AGM), with lovely white flowers which take on a pinkish tinge as they age.

CULTIVATION **Soil type** These plants are happy in most humus-rich, moisture-retentive soils.

Planting Plant either in the autumn or spring, ideally in sun or in a lightly shaded position.

Maintenance Remove any dead leaves in the autumn. A top dressing of well-rotted compost immediately after flowering is beneficial.

Propagation Carefully lift and divide in the spring immediately after flowering: this will give the divisions a chance to recover and flower the following year. Ensure that each section has a good portion of rhizome and foliage. Discard old, woody centre portions.

Pests and diseases Leaf spot fungus can attack foliage. This can be difficult to control – remove infected leaves and spray the plant with mancozeb. Otherwise generally trouble free.

BRUNNERA

COMMON NAME: SIBERIAN BUGLOSS
FAMILY: BORAGINACEAE

These hardy herbaceous plants, with their flowers like forget-me-nots, are excellent for ground cover. Easily grown in moist soil in a shaded spot, even under trees, which makes them particularly useful.

Brunnera 'Hadspen Cream' (AGM); a good ground cover subject with attractive foliage

SPECIES AND VARIETIES

Brunnera macrophylla (AGM) is a native of the western Caucasus. It forms a dense mat of heart-shaped leaves, with sprays of blue flowers appearing in the spring. There are several named varieties – 'Langtrees', sometimes listed as 'Aluminium Spot', has spots of silvery grey on the leaves. One very desirable form is 'Dawson's White' syn. 'Variegata', which has foliage with a white variegation. Another, with cream edging to the leaves which highlights its blue flowers, is 'Hadspen Cream' (AGM).

CULTIVATION

Soil type Happy in most fertile soils provided they are moisture-retentive.

Planting This can be either in the autumn or spring.

Maintenance Little attention required in summer. The foliage of 'Dawson's White' can be damaged by wind. In autumn, cut back dead foliage and tidy.

Propagation Carefully lift and divide in the autumn or early spring, retaining strong outer portions.

Pests and diseases Brunnera are usually trouble free.

CALTHA

COMMON NAMES: KINGCUP, MARSH MARIGOLD
FAMILY: RANUNCULACEAE

These are free-flowering plants for moist, boggy soils, ideally at the edge of a garden pond or stream. *Caltha palustris* (AGM) is one of the most attractive native plants – its gorgeous deep yellow flowers over shiny foliage add a welcome splash of colour to waterside meadows in early spring.

Caltha palustris 'Flore Pleno' (AGM); a moisture lover, early-flowering, with masses of double, golden yellow flowers

SPECIES AND VARIETIES

Caltha palustris has a wide distribution in Europe and North America. It flowers in April. *Caltha palustris* var. *alba*, originating from the Himalayas, will tolerate drier conditions and, unlike the type plant, is not happy growing in shallow water. The most impressive of all is *Caltha palustris* 'Flore Pleno' (AGM), producing masses of bright golden yellow, fully double flowers which can completely hide the shiny foliage. The individual flowers are slightly smaller but are produced in large numbers. The largest member of the family was, for years, listed as *C. polypetala*, a sizable plant which, in ideal conditions, can reach 60cm/24in. It has cheerful golden yellow flowers of 5cm/2in across. This caltha has now been renamed and is to be found listed as *Caltha palustris* var. *palustris*.

CULTIVATION

Soil type Good, humus-rich, boggy or moist soil, in full sun or in lightly shaded areas.

Planting Plant in the spring or early summer. In hot, dry weather ensure plants do not dry out.

Maintenance Very little required except a tidy up in the autumn.

Propagation Lift and divide the plants after flowering. In the case of *Caltha palustris* var. *palustris*, the stems may well root into the soil – simply cut them on either side of the roots and plant into a new position. Calthas, with the exception of the double form, can be grown from seed. This can be sown as soon as ripe or in the following spring. Sow in boxes of John Innes seed compost and place in a cold frame. Prick out when large enough to handle, this time into deeper boxes, making sure that they do not dry out. They can be planted out in the autumn or spring.

Pests and diseases In most years calthas are trouble free, though mildew can sometimes affect foliage, particularly the white forms. Treat with a fungicide when seen.

CAMPANULA

COMMON NAME: BELLFLOWER
FAMILY: CAMPANULACEAE

This is a very large group of plants, including many which are splendid subjects for the border. They are sun lovers of varying shades of blue and pink and also pure white. Campanulas are easily grown; choose a sheltered spot for the taller varieties to avoid damage in heavy rain and wind.

Campanula lactiflora 'Pritchard's Variety' (AGM); a free-flowering, violet blue – one of the finest bellflowers

SPECIES AND VARIETIES

Campanula lactiflora is a native of the Caucasus, a variable plant both in height and colour. Widely available, mostly in shades of lavender blue, also a white form. There are several very desirable named varieties. One of these is the old favourite 'Pritchard's Variety' (AGM), a very free-flowering lavender blue, reaching 1m/3ft in height. 'Loddon Anna' is even taller, with soft pink flowers. In complete contrast, 'Pouffe' grows to just 25cm/10in, making it ideal for the front of the border. 'White Pouffe' grows to the same height. The 'giant bellflower', *Campanula latifolia*, is a tall plant, as its common name indicates, with large, drooping, purple blue bells. It can easily reach 1.5m/5ft. Here again there are several named varieties: 'Brentwood', a rich violet purple, 'Gloaming', a pastel blue (not as frequently seen as it used to be) and 'White Ladies', a very pleasing contrast with its large white bells. One campanula which looks particularly attractive in small groups at the front of a border is

Campanula takesimana; tubular, bell-shaped flowers of lilac white, produced freely

Campanula persicifolia 'Caerulea Plena'; a splendid double form of this well-known, easily grown plant

Campanula glomerata. It is a variable plant ranging in height from 30–90cm/12–36in, with dense heads of violet blue flowers, hence its common name, clustered bellflower. *Campanula glomerata* var. *dahurica* is a vigorous plant with purple flowers, reaching 50cm/20in. 'Superba' (AGM), widely available, has an invasive nature so should be positioned with care. Its rich violet blue flowers are held on 80cm/32in stems. Another campanula which has become popular is *C. takesimana*, a native of Korea. This has arching spikes of 60cm/24in with lilac bells – there is also a white form. One of the best known perennial campanulas for the border is unquestionably *C. persicifolia*, introduced in the sixteenth century, going on to become a plant widely seen in cottage gardens. This grows to 90cm/36in in height. Its wiry stems have narrow leaves and lilac blue, cup-shaped flowers. This, and the white form listed simply as 'Alba', are widely available. There are many named varieties with single and double blooms. 'Telham Beauty' has large, rich blue single flowers and among the doubles are 'Fleur de Neige' (AGM), with white flowers, 'Hampstead White', another good choice with an extra ruff of petals behind the flower, and not forgetting 'Pride of Exmouth' with its light blue flowers. There are many more perennial campanulas, including splendid plants for the rock garden and others which are biennials.

CULTIVATION

Soil type Campanulas will thrive in most fertile, well drained soils, including alkaline, with a few exceptions (mostly alpines), in sun or lightly shaded spots.

Planting This can be done in the autumn or spring.

Maintenance The taller-growing campanulas should be given sheltered positions. They may require supporting by means of twiggy sticks to prevent wind and rain damage. Regular deadheading will usually result in further flowers being produced, especially in the case of *C. persicifolia*, which often self-seeds freely. In the autumn, cut down old stems and tidy up.

Propagation The border perennials can be increased by two methods: by division or by basal cuttings. Divide in the spring, selecting strong outer portions, and replant immediately. Take basal cuttings in the spring, root in an equal peat and sand mixture, and place in a garden frame. Pot into 8cm/3⅛in pots and plant out when well rooted; if ready, in the autumn, if not the following spring.

Pests and diseases The most likely problem to be encountered is slug and snail damage, especially to new growth. Some species can be attacked by a fungal disease which shows as white or brown spots on the foliage; this can be treated with a fungicide.

COREOPSIS

COMMON NAME: TICKSEED
FAMILY: ASTERACEAE

The free-flowering coreopsis are excellent plants for the border. There are two hardy perennial species widely grown in Britain, *Coreopsis grandiflora* and *C. verticillata*. Both have yellow flowers and originate from the United States. They are easily grown sun lovers.

Coreopsis verticillata 'Zagreb'; flowering late in the season, this makes a good plant for the front of the border

It is the named varieties of these plants which are the most widely grown. 'Goldfink' is a good choice, with yellow flowers reaching 30cm/12in in height. 'Grandiflora', sometimes still listed as 'Golden Showers', is much larger and can reach 90cm/36in; this is a fine coreopsis with rich golden yellow flowers. If you are looking for a low-growing plant which smothers itself with tiny yellow daisies for weeks on end, then 'Zagreb' is a good choice, reaching just 15cm/6in in height.

CULTIVATION

Soil type Most fertile, well drained soil in an open, sunny spot.

Planting Autumn or spring.

Maintenance The taller-growing varieties need the support of twiggy branches, especially in exposed spots. Deadhead regularly. Coreopsis soon form sizable clumps and quickly exhaust the soil; regular division every few years is necessary to keep them in good form.

Propagation Lift and divide in the autumn or spring. Select strong outer portions, ensuring that each piece has a number of shoots. Old centre pieces should be thrown away.

Pests and diseases Slugs and snails will attack young growth in the spring. Froghoppers are another pest occasionally seen on these plants. Their presence is easily detected by the frothy substance known as cuckoo spit, which conceals the insect. Spray with insecticide.

CORYDALIS

COMMON NAME: NONE
FAMILY: PAPAVERACEAE

When *Corydalis flexuosa* was introduced a few years ago it soon hit the headlines. This handsome, blue-flowered species has proved so popular that it is now widely available. Many members of this family are alpine or bulbous plants and there are a few which are splendid perennials, unquestionably the one already mentioned being top of the list.

SPECIES AND VARIETIES   Several different forms of *Corydalis flexuosa* are available: the type plant has dark, finely cut foliage and blue-spurred flowers, 'China Blue' has lighter blue flowers. One which has easily recognized leaves with a deep purplish tinge and blue flowers tinged with mauve is listed simply as 'Purple Leaf'. The yellow-flowered *Corydalis lutea* is one of those plants that once you have in the garden you are unlikely to lose. It produces neat, fern-like, slightly shiny green foliage, and from late spring, yellow flowers appear. This corydalis grows in any well drained soil. It self-seeds in profusion and is frequently to be seen growing on old walls. Unwanted plants are easily removed. *Corydalis ochroleuca* is a very similar plant, with creamy white flowers over greyish foliage. Another popular member of the family is *C. cheilanthifolia*. This forms

Corydalis flexuosa 'Purple Leaf'; this easily grown corydalis attracted much attention when it was introduced a few years ago. There are several forms available

tufts of bronze-tinted, finely divided leaves. The long racemes' pale yellow, spurred flowers are carried on long stalks from late spring and during the summer months.

CULTIVATION

Soil type Corydalis will grow in most well drained, humus-rich soils.

Planting This is best done in the spring, choosing an open, sunny or lightly shaded position. *Corydalis cheilanthifolia* requires a moist soil in full sun.

Maintenance Little attention is required. Corydalis do have the habit of self-seeding, so a periodical check to remove any which are growing in unwanted positions may be necessary.

Propagation *Corydalis flexuosa* is best propagated by division immediately after flowering. The other species can be grown from seed. Sow in pans as soon as ripe in John Innes seed compost. Do not let the seedlings become too large or overcrowded before pinching out, as the roots are brittle. Prick out into 8cm/3⅛in pots and grow on. Overwinter in a frame and plant into their permanent positions in the spring. *Corydalis lutea* can be sown direct where it is to flower. Thin later if necessary.

Pests and diseases Corydalis are normally unaffected by pests and diseases.

DELPHINIUM

COMMON NAME: NONE
FAMILY: RANUNCULACEAE

The tall, stately delphiniums, which can grow to 2m/6½ft in height, provide a magnificent display in the summer months – they do, however, require more attention than many other perennials. Staking every spike is important – and certainly well worth the effort – to ensure that the display is not spoilt by wind and rain. There are varieties which are much shorter and more in keeping with today's trend towards smaller gardens. Delphiniums are impressive plants, available in single- and double-flowered varieties in a range of sumptuous colours.

Delphinium 'Summer Skies'; these plants require staking to ensure that the impressive flower spikes are not damaged by wind and rain

SPECIES AND VARIETIES

Over the years several leading nurserymen have been involved with the development of these plants, resulting in plants with flowers ranging from vibrant blues, yellows, whites and violet mauve to almost pink. There is a whole host from which to choose. Varieties in the taller group include 'Blue Nile' (AGM), a mid-blue with contrasting white eye, 'Cressida', a lovely pale blue with distinctive white eye, 'Butterball', an alluring rich cream, and 'Strawberry Fair', a mulberry rose highlighted with a white eye. Among the shorter delphinium is the Belladonna Group, with heights ranging up to 90cm/36in. Regular deadheading will prolong the display of this group which, unless grown in a particularly exposed spot, do not require much support.

Delphinium 'Basil Clitheroe'; one of a number of pure white varieties of these very impressive plants

CULTIVATION

Soil type Most deep, humus-rich, well drained soils.

Planting Choose a sunny spot sheltered from strong winds. They can be planted either in the autumn or spring. Beware of slugs and snails which will attack young growth.

Maintenance Regular removal of dead flower spikes will usually result in further flowers. Tall varieties should be staked in April, dwarf varieties can be supported by twiggy sticks if necessary. In the autumn cut back all dead stems and tidy up.

Propagation There are three methods of increasing stock: by division, by basal cuttings or by seed. Division should be done in the early spring, replanting portions immediately. As soon as the plant is large enough, usually in April, take basal cuttings around 5cm/2in in length. Root in an equal mixture of sand and peat, place in a cold frame, grow on in a nursery bed and plant out in the autumn. For propagation by seed, sow in early spring in John Innes seed compost. When the seedlings are large enough to handle, prick out individually into pots. Plant out in the autumn.

Pests and diseases Unfortunately, slugs and snails are attracted to young growth and can also disfigure older leaves – take precautions against attack early by using a slug and snail killer. There are several fungal diseases which can attack delphiniums, causing the plant to collapse and rot away. Viral diseases, for which there is no cure, and mildew, which can be controlled by a fungicide, can also cause problems.

SPECIES AND VARIETIES	*Digitalis grandiflora* (AGM), which has also been listed as *D. ambigua*, is no stranger to our gardens, having been introduced several centuries ago from its native Greece. This is much smaller than the common purple foxgloves, *D. purpurea*, reaching just 60cm/24in in height, with typical flowers of soft creamy yellow. It is happy in full sun or light shade. *Digitalis lutea* has deeper yellow flowers on slightly taller stems.
CULTIVATION	**Soil type** Most ordinary, fertile, well drained garden soils suit these plants.
	Planting This can be done in early autumn or in spring. Ideally, choose a spot where they are not subjected to a lot of wind.
	Maintenance Foxgloves are prolific self-seeders. Removing dead spikes will help to avoid plants growing in wrong places. In the autumn, cut down any remaining dead spikes and tidy up.
	Propagation Seed is the best method of increasing these plants. Scatter the very fine seed on a prepared seed bed or in a seed tray. Cover with a thin layer of fine soil. When large enough to handle, prick out and grow on in a nursery bed. Plant into flowering positions in the autumn.
	Pests and diseases There is little trouble with these plants, although heavy, wet soil conditions, especially in the winter, can result in crown rot.

DORONICUM

COMMON NAME: LEOPARD'S BANE
FAMILY: ASTERACEAE

The yellow daisies of the doronicums are particularly welcome in spring: they flower long before the majority of border plants. If deadheaded they will often produce further flowers in the autumn.

Doronicum columnae (syn. *D. cordatum*); bright yellow daisies early in the season, usually after the daffodils are just past their best

SPECIES AND VARIETIES One of the most popular is the hybrid (x *excelsum*) 'Miss Mason' (AGM), an old stager. It produces a clump of heart-shaped leaves with scalloped edges. The bright yellow flowers on 45cm/18in stems are produced for several weeks. It is happy in sun or lightly shaded areas. 'Frühlingspracht', sometimes listed as 'Spring Beauty', is a double-flowered variety. It also flowers early, with bright yellow blooms. Another hybrid, it was first introduced nearly 40 years ago.

CULTIVATION **Soil type** They are happy in most fertile, well drained soils.

Planting This can be done in the autumn or spring. In the latter, keep well watered until established.

Maintenance Deadhead plants regularly. In hot, dry weather ensure that they have sufficient water. Lift and divide every three years, immediately after flowering or in the autumn: this will keep them vigorous. In the winter a top dressing of well-rotted compost is beneficial.

Propagation Lift and divide in the autumn, selecting strong outer portions and discarding any old, woody centre pieces. Replant immediately.

Pests and diseases Powdery mildew can be a problem in some seasons. Spray with fungicide.

ECHINACEA

COMMON NAME: CONEFLOWER
FAMILY: ASTERACEAE

These close relatives of the popular rudbeckias also have a prominent cone at the centre of the flower, hence their common name. The flowers in this case are purple, pink and white as opposed to the yellows and oranges of the rudbeckias.

Echinacea purpurea 'Magnus'; flower in close-up showing the prominent orange brown centre boss

Echinacea purpurea 'Magnus'; a sun lover with sizable rose flowers

SPECIES AND VARIETIES   The echinaceas which are normally seen in our gardens are named varieties of *Echinacea purpurea*. These range in height from 90cm/36in to 1.5m/5ft depending on variety. Their mid-green foliage is toothed and rather rough to the touch. The very attractive daisy-like blooms, which appear from June until early autumn, are held on stout stems. *Echinacea purpurea*, a native of North America with large, purple crimson flowers, is widely available. There are a number of named varieties, 'Magnus', with deep pink flowers, and 'Robert Bloom', an intense cerise crimson, among them. 'White Star' and 'White Swan', the latter with a deeper orange cone, are not as eye-catching as the others, but all are fine border plants.

CULTIVATION   **Soil type** Most fertile, well drained soils are suitable.

Planting This can be done in the autumn or spring in an open, sunny spot.

Maintenance There is little to do throughout the year. A mulch of well-rotted compost in the spring is beneficial. Deadhead regularly. Cut down any old stems in the late autumn and tidy the site. Echinaceas have strong stems and seldom need supporting.

Propagation Division of clumps is the usual method, either in the spring or autumn. Select strong outer portions, discard old woody sections, and replant immediately. Echinaceas can also be increased by root cuttings taken in February; root in an equal sand/peat mixture.

Pests and diseases These easily grown plants are generally trouble free. Slugs and snails can attack new growth in early spring.

ECHINOPS

COMMON NAME: GLOBE THISTLE
FAMILY: ASTERACEAE

Clumps of these statuesque, hardy herbaceous perennials look very impressive in the border from midsummer onwards, with their rounded heads of blue, or steely blue, over their coarse, rather spiny foliage.

Echinops ritro (AGM); a sun lover which will thrive in poor soil, commonly known as globe thistle

SPECIES AND VARIETIES   *Echinops ritro* (AGM) can easily reach 1.2m/4ft in good conditions and is particularly useful at the back of a border. There are several named varieties; 'Veitch's Blue' is slightly smaller in flower size and more free-flowering than the type plant. *Echinops bannaticus* is later flowering; their rounded heads of greyish blue flowers on 1.5m/5ft stems make them suitable for the back of a border. One to look out for is 'Taplow Blue', with pale blue flowers up to 7cm/3in across from midsummer through to early autumn.

CULTIVATION   **Soil type**   Most ordinary, fertile, well drained soils in an open, sunny position. They will grow in poor, dry conditions, but will not do as well.

Planting   This can be done in the autumn or spring.

Maintenance   Regular deadheading throughout the season is beneficial. Staking is not required. The foliage is spiny and thistle-like, so it is best to wear gloves when handling. In the autumn, cut the stems down to ground level and tidy the site.

Propagation   As with many hardy herbaceous perennials, division is the usual method of increasing stock, either in the autumn or early spring. Echinops can also be propagated by root cuttings taken in November or December or from seed sown in the spring.

Pests and diseases   Mildew can attack. If this happens during the growing or flowering season it can be treated with a fungicide. After flowering, cut down foliage to the base.

EPILOBIUM

COMMON NAME: WILLOW HERB
FAMILY: ONAGRACEAE

These plants are widely known through our native, very colourful rosebay willow herb, *E. angustifolium*, an invasive, creeping plant which is only suitable for the wild garden where its prolific self-seeding habit will not cause problems. Among this large family are others which are better behaved.

Epilobium angustifolium f. *album*; the pure white form of rosebay willow herb is less invasive than the type plant

SPECIES AND VARIETIES

Epilobium angustifolium, attractive as it is, should be treated with extreme caution. There is also a white form, *E. angustifolium* f. *album*, which is less invasive. The same applies to the pale pink 'Isobel'. The much shorter *E. donanei*, with its mauve pink flowers, grows to 75cm/30in in height and spreads to 60cm/24in. Flowering commences in June and continues for several weeks. This plant is no stranger to our gardens, being first introduced 200 years ago. The leaves are grey green, long and narrow. With a much more compact habit is *E. fleischeri*, often confused with the former. It has rose-coloured flowers over similar foliage and reaches 30cm/12in in height, with well grown specimens just 30cm/12in across. This is a native of southern Europe but can also be found in Britain.

CULTIVATION

Soil type Not fussy – most well drained soils in an open, sunny spot.

Planting Epilobium should be planted in the autumn or spring, or during the winter if the soil conditions are suitable.

Maintenance Deadheading regularly will help to prevent unwanted seedlings. In the autumn cut back dead foliage and tidy the site.

Propagation Epilobiums are easily grown from seed sown in the spring, in trays of John Innes seed compost. Prick out into pots when large enough to handle and grow on. Plant out in the autumn. Another method is by basal cuttings taken in the spring; root in an equal mix of peat and sand, treat as seedlings when rooted.

Pests and diseases Flea beetle can attack foliage; treat with Derris Dust.

EPIMEDIUM

COMMON NAME: BARRENWORT
FAMILY: BERBERIDACEAE

Mostly grown as ground cover plants. Many have very attractive foliage in the spring, others in the autumn and winter. They are moisture lovers and will grow happily in shady spots which do not dry out. Grown primarily for their foliage, the small flowers, held on wiry stems, are also attractive.

Epimedium perralderianum 'Frohnleiten'; useful ground cover plants with attractive leaf colouring in spring and autumn

SPECIES AND VARIETIES One very popular member of the family is *E.* x *rubrum* (AGM). The young foliage is tinged with red and during May, crimson flowers appear. In the autumn this charming plant rewards again – at this time the foliage turns orange and yellow. Another good choice is the semi-evergreen *E. pinnatum* subsp. *colchicum* (AGM), with yellow flowers and red-tinged foliage in the autumn and winter. Many species and forms of these very useful plants are available. One not to overlook is *E. alpinum*, with reddish flowers and good autumn colour.

CULTIVATION **Soil type** Most humus-rich soils are suitable. They prefer moist conditions but are remarkably adaptable and many will grow in much drier conditions.

Planting This can be done in either the autumn or spring. In the latter case, ensure a plentiful supply of moisture until well established. Epimedium grow best in lightly shaded positions.

Maintenance These plants will benefit from a top dressing of leaf mould in the spring. Removal of the leaves of the semi-evergreen varieties in February, before the new foliage and flowers form, is beneficial because it will enable a good show of new foliage.

Propagation Lift and divide the rhizomatous roots in the autumn or spring and replant portions retained immediately. Epimedium can also be increased by seed sown in a garden frame as soon as ripe.

Pests and diseases Sparrows will sometimes attack new flowers in the spring, otherwise they are generally trouble free.

ERIGERON

COMMON NAME: FLEABANE
FAMILY: ASTERACEAE

Erigeron 'Dunkelste Aller' (AGM) (syn. *E.* 'Darkest of All'); a popular variety of these plants

Erigeron 'Unity'; a sun lover which will flower over a long period

These very colourful plants have been a feature of our gardens for a great many years. They have a similarity to the well-known Michaelmas daisies which flower much later. While the species are available, those which appear in our gardens are more likely to be hybrids.

SPECIES AND VARIETIES

Erigeron glaucus, a native of North America, first arrived in Britain in 1812. It is very tolerant of maritime conditions and to this extent can be seen growing on cliffs in the south. The grey green evergreen foliage is, at times, almost hidden by a long succession of mauve daisy-like flowers. 'Elstead Pink' is a good variety, with lilac pink flowers. Many of the erigeron hybrids originated from Bressingham almost 50 years ago. All have been given names ending in 'ity', among them 'Prosperity', a light blue, 'Dignity', lilac, 'Amity', a lilac pink, and 'Charity', a light pink. One of the darkest available is 'Dunkelste Aller' (AGM), for many years listed as 'Darkest of all', a rich violet blue. Look out also for the old favourite 'Foersters Liebling' (AGM) and the lilac 'Rosa Jewel', just two of the numerous varieties available.

CULTIVATION

Soil type Erigeron are easily grown in most moist, well drained soils in an open, sunny position.

Planting This can be done in the autumn, but preferably in the spring, when they will grow away quickly as the soil warms up.

Maintenance Some varieties may need support in the form of twiggy sticks. The usual deadheading will encourage production of further flowers. Cut down to ground level in the autumn.

Propagation Division is the quickest and easiest method of increasing stock. This should be done in the spring.

Pests and diseases New growth in the spring is attractive to slugs and snails – preventive measures should be taken if these pests are a problem (see Chapter 5, page 36).

ERYNGIUM

COMMON NAME: SEA HOLLY
FAMILY: APLACEAE

These very distinctive hardy plants have become very popular. A well grown specimen, with its spiny foliage and branching heads of teasel-like, long-lasting flowers, usually of a bluish almost metallic tinge, stands out well in any border.

Eryngium alpinum (AGM); has the largest flowers of the sea hollies

SPECIES AND VARIETIES

The species producing some of the largest flowers is *Eryngium alpinum* (AGM) which grows to 90cm/36in in height. In June the first of the blue stems carrying the distinctive flower heads lengthen and branch; the steely blue bracts have an attractive ruff. There are a number of named forms varying slightly in colour. The foliage of *E. bourgatti*, a native of the Pyrenees, is deeply cut on the lower leaves, different from those of *E. alpinum* which are grey green with white veining. The flower heads of *E. bourgatti* are blue green. Another good plant is *E.* x *tripartitum* (AGM). This grows to around

75cm/30in and produces, in time, a neat basal rosette of 60cm/24in across. The stems are wiry and carry several branches with blue flower heads surrounded by blue spiky bracts.

CULTIVATION

Soil type Most well drained soils. Overfeeding can result in soft growth.

Planting Choose an open, sunny spot. Place into flowering positions in the autumn or spring. Eryngiums produce long tap roots, so leave undisturbed once planted.

Maintenance Some of the taller varieties will need supporting, especially in exposed positions. Ideally, use twiggy sticks: if used carefully, these will not distract from the flowers themselves. Regular deadheading is beneficial – remember to wear gloves to protect your hands from their spiky foliage. Eryngiums are good for drying; cut before they fade. The seed heads can also be left on the plants over winter.

Propagation Take root cuttings in late winter, root in equal quantities of sand/peat mix and place in a cold frame. Move into flowering positions in the autumn. Eryngiums, which form clumps, can be divided in early spring. Seed of several species is obtainable – sow in a tray of John Innes seed compost in the spring and place in a frame. Prick out when large enough to handle and grow on, ready for planting out in October.

Pests and diseases Blackfly can attack the new growth of some eryngiums in the spring. Spray with insecticides as soon as seen.

EUPATORIUM

COMMON NAME: BONE SET
FAMILY: ASTERACEAE

The moisture-loving *Eupatorium purpureum* is a very impressive plant for the back of a border where, in ideal conditions, it can easily reach 2m/6½ft or more. It flowers in early autumn making it particularly useful, as most of the perennials which bloom in early summer are then long past their best.

SPECIES AND VARIETIES

Eupatorium purpureum is a native of North America where it is widely known as joe-pye weed. It was first introduced into Britain as long ago as 1640. Growing to 2m/6½ft or more, it must be positioned with care. The purplish stems carry whorls of pointed leaves and the tiny, fluffy, rose purple flowers are in dense, flat heads. There are several named forms, of which 'Atropurpureum' (AGM), with purple foliage, is widely available. Not so often seen is the white form, 'Album'.

CULTIVATION

Soil type Most humus-rich, moisture-retentive soils are suitable.

Planting As with so many hardy perennials, it can be planted in the autumn or spring, either in an open, sunny spot or a lightly shaded area.

Maintenance There is little work required during the growing season, except

Eupatorium purpureum; a tall moisture lover, ideal for the back of a border or at the water's edge

watering during any hot, dry spell. Eupatorium does not need staking except in very exposed areas. In late autumn, cut down dead foliage and tidy the site.

Propagation Lift and divide the clumps in the autumn or early spring, retain strong outer portions and replant immediately.

Pests and diseases These are ideal plants for gardeners as they are usually pest and disease free.

EUPHORBIA

COMMON NAME: SPURGE
FAMILY: EUPHORBIACEAE

These are very useful plants for the border. Many have colourful sulphur yellow bracts which surround the insignificant flowers. One notable exception is the popular *E. griffithii* 'Fireglow' which, as its name indicates, has bracts of a fiery orange. Euphorbias are easy to grow – most are sun lovers which do well in light soil. When cut, bruised or damaged a white sap is produced; this can irritate the skin and is very painful if it comes in contact with the eyes, so it is best to wear gloves when handling euphorbias.

Euphorbia characias 'Spring Splendour'; evergreen foliage and tall spikes of yellow green in the spring

Euphorbia griffithii 'Fireglow'; vivid brick red flowers from late spring onwards

SPECIES AND VARIETIES

One of the best known is *E. polychroma* (AGM), a very colourful, spring-flowering plant with bright yellow bracts on 45cm/18in stems. In a comparatively short time it will build up into a sizable clump, the foliage almost completely obscured when in full flower. Taller generally, and with bracts of sulphur yellow, is *E. palustris* (AGM), reaching 90cm/36in. *Euphorbia characias* is a Mediterranean native – an evergreen with shiny foliage. The flower heads, on strong 90cm/36in stems, consist of many small, greenish yellow bracts. There are a number of named forms, including 'Burrow Silver' with creamy edges to the leaves, and 'Lambrook Gold' (AGM), with large flower heads of golden yellow. Look out for 'Spring Splendour' and 'Humpty Dumpty'. 'Variegata' is less vigorous and requires winter protection except in very sheltered spots. The varieties of *E. griffithii*, with orange red bracts, are particularly effective. Two which can be relied upon to provide a colourful display are 'Dixter' (AGM) and 'Fireglow', with its fiery orange bracts. These do best in full sun and good fertile soil. The 90cm/36in flowering stems often don't need supporting, but if necessary in exposed spots, use twiggy sticks.

CULTIVATION

Soil type Light soils generally, with the exception of *E. griffithii*, which prefers more humus-rich conditions.

Planting Plant in the autumn or spring, preferably in spring which will enable quick establishment as the soil warms up. Euphorbia resent root disturbance; choose young, vigorous stock and leave undisturbed once planted.

Maintenance Remove dead flower stems regularly to prevent too much self-seeding. In the autumn, cut back dead foliage of the non-evergreen varieties. Euphorbias start to produce new shoots early in the year; take care not to damage these when working on the border.

Propagation There are three methods; seed sown in pans of John Innes compost in the spring, basal cuttings taken in the spring, and division in early autumn or spring.

Pests and diseases Euphorbias are normally trouble free.

HARDY GERANIUMS

COMMON NAME: CRANESBILL
FAMILY: GERANIACEAE

There are in the region of 400 species of these free-flowering plants, some of which have been grown in our gardens for a great many years. Hardy geraniums have seen a tremendous upsurge in popularity to the extent that they now rate among the most popular of all hardy perennials. They are, by and large, sun lovers and will grow in most fertile soils, with the exception of cold, boggy conditions – a few are best in lightly shaded spots. They have many uses in the garden, among them subjects for the border, for the rock garden or for ground cover. These include the sizzling magenta of *Geranium psilostemon* (AGM) through to delicate blues and pure white. They have a long flowering period and a wide variety of colours.

Geranium psilostemon (AGM); with its brilliant magenta flowers, it must be positioned with care to avoid colour clashes

SPECIES AND VARIETIES Where better than to start with a low-growing species, and one which occurs in this country, *Geranium sanguineum*, which forms low mats of small, divided, rounded leaves in the autumn, taking on many beautiful tints of red, orange and brown. This species has purple magenta flowers of 2.5cm/1in across, produced in large numbers for a long period – a splendid subject for the front of a border, rock garden or bank where it can trail down. It is happy in full sun or partially shaded spots. Many years ago, a distinctive form was found growing on Walney Island, at that time part of Lancashire, now Cumbria. It has graceful, light pink flowers, delicately veined with a deeper pink. For years listed as *G. s.* var. *lancastriense*, and still known to many gardeners by this name, the correct name is now *G. s.* var. *striatum* (AGM).

There are a considerable number of cultivars available, among them 'Glenluce', with rose pink flowers, which was discovered in 1937 near the Scottish town of that name, and 'Shepherd's Warning' (AGM), introduced by Jack Drake, the well-known Scottish nurseryman. One which can usually be relied upon for good autumn leaf colour is 'Max Frei', introduced from Germany and currently widely available. *Geranium sylvaticum* is another plant which is to be found in Europe. One of the best forms is the lovely 'Mayflower' (AGM), a rich violet blue with white eye. Grown in a border in good humus-rich soil, it will flower in early summer; if cut back, it can usually be relied upon to produce a second flush of flowers later in the season.

There are a number of hardy geraniums with bright magenta flowers. One of these is *G. psilostemon* (AGM), a native of north-eastern Turkey and Armenia. This can easily reach 1.2m/4ft in height, so should be placed at the back of a border in full sun or light shade. The flowers of brilliant magenta, with a black eye and veining, are produced during June and July over large, deeply cut leaves, which themselves add colour to the border in the autumn by turning red. This plant looks particularly effective against a background of silver foliage. Another superb hardy geranium, this time with trailing stems, is 'Ann Folkard' (AGM), a hybrid between *G. psilostemon* and *G. procurrens*, introduced 25 years ago. The flowers are freely produced for weeks on end, a magenta purple, again with black veining and central zone. There are four very beautiful varieties with the prefix 'Kashmir'. My favourite has to be 'Kashmir Purple', a vigorous plant with underground rhizomes. The large, upward-facing flowers are a deep violet purple veined with lilac pink, 4cm/1½in across. 'Kashmir Pink' originated as a seedling of the former; it is a much more recent introduction, with soft pink flowers. These two and 'Kashmir White' (AGM) are cultivars of *G. clarkei*. The fourth, 'Kashmir Blue', is a very desirable plant with soft pale blue flowers. It is a hybrid between *G. c.* 'Kashmir White' and *G. pratense* f. *albiflorum*, which was raised nearly 20 years ago in Belgium. One splendid hybrid hardy geranium, which made its debut around 100 years ago, is the rich violet, darkly veined, *G. x magnificum* (AGM), a free-flowering, sterile hybrid of *G. ibericum* and *G. platypetalum*. The saucer-shaped flowers appear in early summer on strong, 30cm/12in stems, over clumps of rounded, hairy foliage. One of the most rewarding members of the family, ideal for a border in full sun or light shade, it is sometimes sold under the name of either parent.

Among our most attractive native plants is *Geranium pratense*. It can often be seen on roadside verges and waste ground. While this is a worthwhile garden plant, it is best restricted to the wild garden due to its free-seeding habit. There are some very desirable garden forms. High in the list is the pale violet blue, white veined 'Mrs Kendall Clark' (AGM). This usually requires some support – in the form of short pea sticks – to keep it tidy, unless grown in a position where strong neighbouring plants provide support. There are double-flowering forms and as these are sterile, they do not present the problems which can be caused by prolific self-seeding. The one most widely grown is *G. plenum* 'Violaceum', a very handsome rich violet with darker centre.

Geranium 'Johnson's Blue' (AGM); free-flowering and covered with flowers in early summer

Geranium x *magnificum* (AGM); a colourful hybrid which has been in gardens for well over 100 years

Another very popular species is *Geranium phaeum*, with dark maroon, almost black, flattish, nodding, reflexed flowers, which is widely known as 'Mourning Widow' due to this sombre colour. There is also a white form listed simply as *G. phaeum* 'Album'. In addition, there are a number of named varieties. Two which are available from many sources are 'Lily Lovell', with large, rich mauve flowers over light green foliage, and 'Taff's Jester', a garden discovery with similar flower colour to the type plant. The foliage of 'Taff's Jester' is mottled with deep yellow and this, coupled with blotching of yellowish green and dark purple brown in the leaf notches, adds up to very attractive foliage.

CULTIVATION

Soil type These easy-going plants will grow well in many well drained soil types. Avoid waterlogged sites. Heavy ground can be improved by adding compost and sharp grit.

Planting Hardy geraniums can be planted in early autumn or spring; in cold gardens the latter is preferable. Prepare the site with the addition of well-rotted compost: this will ensure a good start. Make sure plants do not suffer from drought in any hot, dry weather until well established.

Maintenance Plants will benefit from a light sprinkling of slow-release fertilizer in the spring. Some of the taller varieties may need supporting. Regular cutting back of old flowering stems, ideally done before the seed ripens, will prolong the flowering season. In the autumn, tidy up.

Propagation Division is the usual method of increasing stock, either in the autumn or early spring. Regular dividing every three years or so will keep the plants vigorous and free-flowering, especially with *Geranium phaeum*. This has rhizomatous roots which, after a number of years, deteriorate. Do not be tempted to over-divide; while they will grow well, they naturally take time to build up in size. Select strong outer portions and replant immediately. If replanting in the same spot, rejuvenate the soil.

Pests and diseases Generally, very few problems are encountered with hardy geraniums. Slugs and snails can damage new growth in the spring. One pest which seems to have become more common in recent years is vine weevil – the grubs can attack many plants. Often the first signs of attack are yellowing or sickly plants. At the worst, weevil attack can lead to complete collapse. One very efficient method of control is to use a natural predator, in this case a harmless nematode. It is essential to follow instructions carefully as soil temperature is important. In dry weather, and also when plants are grown in overcrowded conditions, powdery mildew can occur. Cut back and destroy foliage, spray remainder with a fungicide and feed plants – they should soon produce new growth. Unfortunately this troublesome disease can recur.

GEUM

COMMON NAME: AVENS
FAMILY: ROSACEAE

These are among the most effective plants for the front of a border. With their brightly coloured flowers, they need to be positioned with care, especially those with red and orange blooms. They look best in small groups. Regular division every few years is necessary to keep them healthy and flowering freely.

Geum 'Borisii' growing next to a hardy geranium. This hybrid is a good ground cover plant which also has the advantage of eye-catching orange flowers

SPECIES AND VARIETIES   The most popular members of this family are hybrids. One of the best is the brick red, semi-double 'Mrs. J. Bradshaw' (AGM). Other good choices are 'Lady Stratheden' (AGM), another semi-double with warm yellow flowers, and 'Fire Opal' (AGM), an old stager with orange blooms which was introduced over 70 years ago.

CULTIVATION   **Soil type** Most fertile garden soils are suitable.

Planting Geums are best in a sunny spot or lightly shaded area. Planting can be done in the autumn or spring.

Maintenance Keep up the deadheading throughout the long flowering season: this will encourage more flowers. Tidy up in the autumn.

Propagation Lift in early spring and carefully divide. Throw away old, woody centre portions and replant the vigorous outer sections immediately.

Pests and diseases Towards the end of the season geums may be attacked by mildew. Spray with fungicide and cut back any badly affected foliage.

GYPSOPHILA

COMMON NAME: BABY'S BREATH
FAMILY: CAROPHYLLACEAE

The perennial *Gypsophila paniculata* is another plant which has been grown for a great many years. During that time it has become a firm cottage garden favourite. It is a sun lover which, when left undisturbed, will produce a sizable plant of 1.2m/4ft across with a mass of tiny, frothy flowers.

Gypsophila paniculata 'Compacta Plena' forms a sizable mound and masses of frothy flowers

SPECIES AND VARIETIES | *Gypsophila paniculata* is a native of Eastern Europe. It is a good plant to place behind spring-flowering bulbs as it will usually cover any bare spaces left after they have died back. There are a number of named variates; the pure white 'Bristol Fairy' (AGM) is still as popular as ever since being introduced in 1928. 'Compacta Plena' is another good choice, with tiny double flowers. Look out also for the pale pink 'Flamingo'.

CULTIVATION | **Soil type** Gypsophilas grow best in deeply cultivated, slightly alkaline soil. On acid conditions lime should be added.

Planting Plant in the autumn or spring. Once planted leave undisturbed: they produce a tap root so will not move successfully.

Maintenance Some of the taller species can be damaged by strong winds – support in the form of twiggy sticks is usually sufficient.

Propagation Seed can be sown in the spring, in pots containing John Innes seed compost, and transferred later to an outdoor seed bed. Plant into their permanent positions in the autumn or following spring. Another method of increasing stock is by basal cuttings of around 6–7cm/2½–3in in length, taken in the spring. Root in an equal mix of peat and sand and when well rooted, transfer to a nursery bed. Plant out in the autumn or spring.

Pests and diseases Generally trouble free, they can be attacked by stem rot. Lift and burn any infected plants and find a different spot in the garden for any replacements.

HELENIUM

COMMON NAME: SNEEZEWEED
FAMILY: ASTERACEAE

Despite its rather unfortunate common name, helenium are excellent perennials, flowering in midsummer and usually on into early autumn.

SPECIES AND VARIETIES | It is the named varieties which are the most popular. There are a considerable number available. Among the first to flower are 'Crimson Beauty', opening its first mahogany brown flowers in June, and 'Coppelia', a lovely, sturdy, coppery orange plant. Both grow to around 60–70cm/24–27in. Certainly one of the most popular is 'Moerheim Beauty', with its bronze red flowers – at their best in July and August – held on 1m/3ft stems. 'Wyndley' is another good choice, a mixture of yellow and copper reaching 60cm/24in.

CULTIVATION | **Soil type** Heleniums are easily grown in good, moisture-retentive soils, in an open, sunny position. Dry conditions will lead to smaller flowers.

Planting As with many hardy perennials, planting can be carried out in the autumn or spring.

Helenium 'Wyndley'; a compact variety of this popular plant which flowers over a long period

Maintenance Heleniums require a plentiful supply of moisture in hot, dry weather. If the plants are short of water, this is quickly indicated by drooping leaves. Deadhead regularly: this will encourage the early flowering varieties to produce more blooms later. Lift and divide every three years to retain vigour and to prevent congestion. In the autumn cut down old foliage and tidy up. Top dressing in the spring, with well-rotted compost, is beneficial.

Propagation Lift and divide in the autumn or spring.

Pests and diseases Beware of slug damage to new growth in the spring. It is advisable to take precautions if these are a problem in your garden.

HELIANTHUS

COMMON NAME: SUNFLOWER
FAMILY: ASTERACEAE

Recent years have seen the annual sunflower, *Helianthus annus*, become very popular both for colour in the garden and as cut flowers. Fortunately, there are some very useful perennials, not as large and flamboyant as the annuals, but nevertheless, ideal subjects for providing colour in the border from midsummer onwards.

SPECIES AND VARIETIES

Helianthus decapetalus is a native of the United States and was first introduced to Britain around the middle of the eighteenth century. The most popular today are hybrids. Among those to look out for are 'Capenock Star' (AGM), with single, lemon yellow blooms on sturdy 1.2m/4ft stems, 'Loddon Gold' (AGM), a double, rich golden yellow which grows to 1.5m/5ft, making it an ideal subject for the back of the border, and 'Soleil d'Or', a real old stager which made its debut well over 100 years ago.

CULTIVATION

Soil type These plants are easy to grow in good, fertile garden soil which is moisture-retentive and well drained. As their name implies, they are sun lovers. Beware of overfeeding, which results in more foliage and less flowers.

Planting This can be done either in the autumn or spring.

Maintenance Ensure a plentiful supply of water in dry weather. The taller varieties may need supporting. Deadhead regularly. Lift and divide every three years to control their spreading. This will also prevent the double-flowered varieties reverting to singles, which can sometimes happen if left too long.

Propagation Lift and divide clumps in the autumn or early spring. Select strong outer portions and replant immediately.

Pests and diseases Slugs can attack new growth in the spring. In wet weather botrytis (grey mould) can be a problem; badly affected plants should be burnt, spray others with fungicide. Mildew is another disease which can be a nuisance in dry summers. Wherever possible, try to ensure that air can circulate around the plants.

Helianthus decapetalus 'Morning Sun'; a semi-double member of the sunflower family

HELLEBORUS

COMMON NAME: HELLEBORE
FAMILY: RANUNCULACEAE

Winter still has to release its grip when the first buds on hellebores start to expand. At this time spring seems a long way ahead as often, more cold, damp, dismal conditions are to come. 'Christmas Rose' and 'Lenten Rose' are two widely known common names. Hellebores are addictive, such is their magic, especially the 'Orientalis hybrids', with their wide range of colours and forms. These are by no means the only members of the family; our own native hellebore, *H. foetidus*, commonly known as the stinking hellebore due to the rather unpleasant smell produced when the foliage is damaged, is a very useful plant for lightly shaded areas.

Helleborus orientalis; the dark, almost black varieties of this species are very popular

SPECIES AND VARIETIES

Among the first hellebore to flower is the *H. niger* (Christmas rose). This is an evergreen with dark green leathery leaves. The sizable, flat white flowers are carried on strong, 22cm/9in stems from January onwards. There are a number of very desirable forms, among them 'White Magic', with a brighter green foliage. 'Louis Cobbett' has pink buds opening to flowers flushed with pink on the back. 'Trotter's Form' has large, pure white flowers. There are a number with green flowers. One of these is *Helleborus argutifolius*, formerly known as *H. corsicus*, a very attractive plant reaching 90cm/36in, with spiny, divided leaves. The green, cup-shaped flowers appear from January onwards. *Helleborus foetidus* also has green flowers. A taller plant, it can reach 1.2m/4ft in ideal conditions. Among the named forms is 'Wester Flisk', with reddish stems. It originates from the place after which it is named on the Firth of Tay.

Another early flowering plant is *H. purpurascens*, which dies down for the winter. The flower buds can start to appear as early as December, and open to dull purple flowers on 22cm/9in stems which are at their best in March. The most popular hellebores are those known as the Oriental Hybrids, with a great many named varieties in a wide range of colours from almost black to purple, pink, yellow and white, some with plain flowers, others spotted and veined. It is best to see them in flower before making a choice.

CULTIVATION

Soil type These plants will grow in many soils but ideally, humus-rich, with neutral or slightly alkaline conditions, which does not become too dry in the summer or waterlogged during the winter.

Helleborus orientalis; superb for a moist, lightly shaded spot

Planting Most hellebores will grow satisfactorily in full sun or light shade. They are hardy, long-lived plants which should not be disturbed. Avoid spots where they are subjected to strong, cold winds. Do not plant too closely together: the Orientalis Hybrids will, in time, produce sturdy clumps, so it is best to allow 1m/3ft between each plant. Planting is best in the autumn but pot-grown plants can be planted in the spring.

Maintenance Ensure that newly planted hellebores do not dry out in hot spells. Mulching with compost or bark will help to conserve moisture. Keep an eye open for pests and diseases. Remove dead flower stems. There is little other general work during the year.

Propagation Division after flowering, in the case of *H. niger* and the Orientalis Hybrids at the end of August, just as root growth begins. Some, including *H. argutifolius* and *H. foetidus*, are best raised from seed as variations will be slight. The seed of hellebores should be sown as soon as possible after collection, in pots containing John Innes seed compost. Cover with a layer of coarse grit and place in a garden frame – ensure that the seeds do not dry out. Seedlings will start to appear from October onwards; beware of slugs and snails at this stage. Prick out into 7cm/3in pots in the spring when large enough to handle. Plant into their flowering positions in the autumn. Many hellebores will self-seed – it is worth checking periodically.

Pests and diseases Aphids can be a problem; keep a careful watch and spray with insecticide if seen. Slugs and snails will attack new growth. A fungal disease can also attack the foliage and flowers of hellebores. This appears initially as black or brown blotches. These eventually develop into dead patches which may, in turn, cause leaves to die. Remove any infected foliage and spray well with a systemic fungicide.

HEMEROCALLIS

Common name: Daylily
Family: Hemerocallidaceae

The flamboyant day lilies are, unquestionably, among the most popular hardy perennials. A staggering number of cultivars are registered – numbering many thousands – with each year seeing additions to the formidable lists. Today there are daylilies suitable for all gardens, ranging from the large-flowered types, which are by far the most numerous, to the small-flowered, with individual blooms between 7.5–11cm/3–4½in, to the miniatures, with flowers of less than 7.5cm/3in. The small-flowered and miniatures are splendid plants for today's smaller gardens or for growing in containers. There is also a fourth group, the unusual-flowered and spider forms, mostly grown by enthusiasts. The kaleidoscope of colours available ranges from rich reds, oranges and glowing purples, through yellows, creams, apricots, golds and browns. There are also lovely pinks and lavenders to a near black, many with trumpet flowers, while others are peony-shaped or have ruffled petals and bold eye colours, with countless variations. No matter whether your preference is for strong, hot colours or delicate pastel shades, they can all be found in daylilies.

Hemerocallis 'Stafford'; an old stager maybe, but still one of the best reds

Hemerocallis are native to Asia. The first species are thought to have arrived in Europe during the sixteenth century. It was not until the late nineteenth century that hybrids started to make their appearance and many of these early introductions have now been lost. In the early years of the twentieth century, hybrids were the work of two breeders, later joined by others in Great Britain, the United States and Europe, with hybrids being introduced at an ever-increasing rate. Their common name, daylily, should in no way put anyone off these very attractive plants. While individual flowers do last for just one day, they are produced in large numbers, with established plants continuing the show for several weeks.

SPECIES AND VARIETIES

Although not as often seen in our gardens, the species have their own attraction. By far the most popular is *Hemerocallis lilioasphodelus* (syn. *H. flava*) (AGM). This has several common names, the best-known being lemon daylily. A free-flowering species occurring over a wide area, it was among the first to reach Europe over 400 years ago. The clear yellow, fragrant, lily-shaped flowers appear in late spring over narrow, upright foliage. The grass-leaved daylily, *Hemerocallis minor*, is a native of eastern Asia, introduced in the mid-1700s. It has yellow flowers with a brownish tinge to the outer petals, on 45cm/18in stems. Making its appearance around the same time was *Hemerocallis fulva*, a native of Japan. This is a vigorous plant with variable flower colouring, usually an orange red. There are two double forms; 'Flore Pleno' has hose-in-hose blooms with a distinctive red eye, and 'Kwanso Variegata', as its name implies, has variegated foliage and slightly darker flowers. A number of other species are available, generally sought by hardy-plant enthusiasts. For the majority of gardeners it is the very colourful hybrids that have the most appeal.

Hybrids As already mentioned, the choice and range is tremendous. Short of a seemingly endless list, it is best to restrict the large-flowered varieties to just 10. One mahogany red which has stood the test of time well is 'Stafford'; slightly lighter is the dazzling red 'Alan'. Another with strong colour – and broad petals – is the vigorous, orange yellow 'Chicago Sunrise'. A pure yellow which can certainly be relied upon to provide a fine show is 'Lark Song'. Another old favourite, with delicate, primrose yellow flowers and a lime shading to the throat, is 'Whichford'. Among the many bicolours is the bright, orange yellow and brick red 'Frans Hals', not a newcomer but still as popular as ever. The pastel shades of hemerocallis are particularly attractive; 'Catherine Woodbury' is a splendid choice, with soft pink flowers highlighted by a lime green throat. Another strong grower is 'George Cunningham', best described as a melon pink. One which is sure to attract attention is the elegant 'Varsity', a creamy peach with a handsome maroon eye and lime green throat. If asked which variety I would choose to round off these 10 daylilies, it would have to be 'Burning Daylight', its sumptuous, rich deep orange flowers will certainly liven up any border.

Small and miniature daylilies Almost certainly, in any list of these plants, you will find some with the Siloam prefix to their name. These are the work of Pauline Henry of Siloam Springs in the United States, who has introduced over 300. 'Siloam Ury Winniford' made its debut in 1980, a rich ivory with ruffled petals and deep claret eye. Others to look out for in this group are 'Corky', introduced in 1959, with bell-shaped yellow flowers and a brown back to the petals, and 'Golden Chimes', a vigorous, free-flowering variety with gorgeous, golden yellow, bell-shaped flowers on 65cm/25½in stems; both were raised in Germany. A more recent introduction is the prolific 'Cranberry Baby', another vigorous grower, whose name perfectly describes the flower colour, cranberry red. All of the plants listed here are obtainable from many sources. Daylilies can be addictive – hardly surprising with such a range of graceful flowers – so be warned. Several nurseries list more recent introductions, many of which originate from the United States where they have a strong following.

CULTIVATION   **Soil type** These are easy-going hardy perennials which will grow successfully in many soil types, ideally humus-rich, well cultivated and drained. Heavy soils can be improved by the addition of plenty of coarse grit and well-rotted

Hemerocallis 'Lark Song'; an old favourite with clear canary yellow flowers

compost. Avoid cold, wet conditions which can result in the loss of plants through rotting. Light, sandy soils should be improved by digging in plenty of well-rotted organic matter. The free draining of this type of soil results in nutrients being leached out quickly.

Planting Given the choice, spring planting is best, especially in cold areas. Plants will establish quickly and make good roots before winter. Always ensure a plentiful supply of water during hot, dry weather. Daylilies can also be planted in the autumn, ideally while the soil is still warm and several weeks before the first sharp frosts. Dig out a hole to twice the size of the plant's roots, incorporating well-rotted compost. Plant the crown at the same level as it was originally. Once in its permanent position, leave undisturbed to produce a sizable clump. Spacing 60–90cm/24–36in apart will give plenty of room for the hemerocallis to remain in the same place for several years. They can be as close as 45cm/18in, but while this will provide a bolder display of colour more quickly, it will be necessary to lift and divide the plants in a few years, as overcrowding will eventually, and invariably, lead to poor flowering. Daylilies require an open, sunny position and are not successful in shady spots.

Maintenance An annual mulch of well-rotted garden or old mushroom compost, applied in the autumn, is beneficial after the foliage has died down. Foliar feeding every three weeks with a well-balanced fertilizer is useful. Commence in late spring and continue until the flower buds start to form. Daylilies require a plentiful supply of moisture during the growing season:

dryness at the roots can lead to poor foliage, less flowers blooming and a shorter flowering period. In the autumn, remove dead leaves and old flower stems.

Propagation Unless additional plants are required, it is best to leave clumps untouched for four to five years. Division is the best method of propagation and can be done in the autumn or spring. Carefully lift the clumps and divide – it is likely that two garden forks, back-to-back and prising apart in the usual manner, will be necessary on old clumps. Do not divide to single fans; the divisions should consist of two or more, ensuring that each has strong roots. These can be shortened to about half their length, which will encourage the production of new, vigorous roots. Replant immediately, ideally in a fresh spot. If the same position is to be used, the soil should be rejuvenated with compost and a balanced fertilizer.

Hemerocallis 'Graceful Eye'; there are hundreds of these very colourful plants from which to make your selection

Pests and diseases Hemerocallis are generally trouble free. Slugs and snails can become a nuisance, attacking fresh growth in the spring.

HOSTA

COMMON NAME: PLANTAIN LILY
FAMILY: HOSTACEAE

These elegant plants are among the most popular of all hardy perennials. They are grown principally for their handsome foliage, which is produced in a range of shapes, sizes and colours. In the summer they produce strong stems with mostly trumpet-shaped flowers, varying from pale lilac or mauve to white. Leaf size is equally variable, from those with huge leaves of 30cm/12in or more to the small-leaved varieties of just 5cm/2in. One of the main attractions is the diverse colour range of their foliage, with greens, golds and blues, many with cream or white margins to the leaves. Hostas are found in various parts of Asia, with many native to Japan and China. In the region of 70 varieties are known, with over 1,000 cultivars, each year seeing more added to the already formidable list. These very attractive plants will thrive in sun or light shade. They are moisture lovers. If grown in any sunny position, a plentiful supply of moisture will be required. Provided this is available, they will form compact plants and produce more flowers than if grown in partial shade. If grown in partial shade, individual leaves may be larger and flower stems taller. Hostas are excellent plants beside a pond or stream where they will enjoy the cool, moist conditions and humid atmosphere. They will not survive in cold, wet soils so they should not, under any circumstances, be planted in a bog garden.

Hostas are another of those plants which are addictive. Many gardeners go on to form sizable collections, eagerly scanning catalogues and flower shows for new introductions to add to those they already have. Indeed, there are several nurserymen specializing in these plants. In recent years there has been a tremendous upsurge in patio gardening – hostas are ideal plants for pots and containers. When grown in this manner they should be planted in a soil-based compost; other types dry out too quickly. Watering is important, especially in hot weather. Keep the compost moist and, if possible, keep the plant in shade during the hottest part of the day. Feeding can commence from when they start into growth until the end of June, using a soluble, well-balanced general fertilizer. Alternatively, feeding can commence in early spring, with a pelleted slow-release product.

SPECIES AND VARIETIES   *Hosta fortunei* var. *albopicta* (AGM) has become a great favourite with its long, heart-shaped, creamy yellow leaves with deep green margins, and pale mauve flowers carried on 75cm/30in stems. The foliage generally fades to a

Hosta 'Tall Boy'; mid-green shiny leaves and noted for its tall stems of purple flowers

Hosta fortunei var. *aureomarginata* requires a lightly shaded spot in cool, humus-rich, moist soil

Hostas are very popular and are grown mainly for their attractive foliage

mid-green from early summer onwards. *Hosta fortunei* var. *aureomarginata* (AGM) is a splendid plant with large, heart-shaped, olive green, veined foliage attractively edged with light yellow. The flowers are a slightly darker shade of mauve. There is a third award holder: *H. f.* var. *hyacinthina*, which has greyish green leaves highlighted by a white margin. The deep mauve flowers are produced freely on strong stems held well clear of the foliage.

With a vast choice of varieties available, making a selection is really a matter of personal preference so I propose to mention just a few, all well known, which are available from many sources. Firstly, 'Frances Williams', with lovely shiny, heart-shaped, blue grey, puckered leaves, broadly margined with striking yellow. This was introduced from the United States, originally under the name 'Gold Edge'. Another American introduction, which has been available for over 30 years, is 'Gold Standard' (AGM). This has heart-shaped, rich green, veined leaves with wavy edges. It is a later-flowering variety with ivory white, slightly fragrant blooms. There are a considerable number with blue green foliage, one of which is 'Hadspen Blue' and another worth looking out for, 'Blue Moon', both raised in Britain. Among the most attractive hostas are those with shiny, dark green foliage and a distinctive creamy white margin. One such is 'Wide Brim' (AGM), a splendid variety for the garden or containers. Two with very large leaves, albeit with different leaf colouring, are 'Big Daddy' with substantial, puckered, heart-shaped, shiny blue leaves, and the lovely golden yellow 'Zounds', with an almost metallic sheen to the foliage. Both have pale mauve flowers.

CULTIVATION

Soil type Hostas are easily grown in good, moist, humus-rich soil. On sandy soil, enrich with well-rotted compost.

Planting This can be in the autumn, but ideally in early spring when the plants are still dormant, with the tips just below soil level. Hostas are usually sold container-grown. These can be planted at other times but not in high summer. Always ensure a plentiful supply of moisture until well established. Once planted, leave undisturbed to build up sizable clumps.

Maintenance For successful growth, hostas require a plentiful supply of water. When watering, it is best not to wet the foliage: this can cause unsightly marks and scorching. In hot weather water thoroughly. An annual winter mulch of well-rotted compost is beneficial. In the spring, apply a light dressing of general fertilizer, working it into the soil but taking care not to damage young growth. In autumn, clear away dead leaves and any debris which could harbour pests.

Propagation In early spring, carefully lift established clumps and divide. It may be necessary to use two forks back-to-back. Select sections of several young shoots and replant. Unless you require a large number of plants, avoid the temptation to divide to single shoots: these will grow, providing sufficient roots are attached, but will take some time to produce sizable plants. Hostas are reasonably easy to raise from seed but these will not come true.

Pests and diseases Any display of hostas can be quickly ruined by slugs and snails. They will attack young growth in the spring with the result that the foliage will be spoilt for the year. Take precautions by using one of the proprietary slug killers or a nematode treatment. Another pest which can cause great damage, especially when plants are grown in pots and containers, is the grub of the vine weevil. The most effective method of prevention and treatment is to use a nematode preparation. These will seek out and destroy any grubs. It is most important to use as per suppliers instructions, and soil temperature at the time of application is important.

INULA

COMMON NAME: NONE
FAMILY: ASTERACEAE

There are several species of these easily grown yellow daisies in cultivation, two of which are more commonly seen. One of these, impressive in flower with stems reaching 2m/6½ft, has broad, rough foliage that needs a lot of space; this makes it suitable for large gardens only.

SPECIES AND VARIETIES

Inula hookeri is a native of the Himalayas, first introduced in the nineteenth century. A sun lover, it is a good border plant, flowering in late summer and early autumn when many perennials are past their best. A bushy plant with

Inula hookeri; a native of the Himalayas, this is a vigorous plant which enjoys moist conditions

rather coarse, soft and hairy, oval mid-green leaves, the individual flowers, 8cm/3in across, are pale yellow, slightly fragrant, and with narrow petals. The plant mentioned previously as suitable for larger gardens is *I. magnifica*, a native of the Caucasus, introduced to Britain in 1925. This can easily reach 2m/6½ft when grown with a plentiful supply of moisture at the side of a stream or pond. The brown flower buds and stems carry bright yellow daisies in late August, with individual flowers up to 15cm/6in across.

CULTIVATION

Soil type Inulas will thrive in most moisture-retentive soil.

Planting These are sun lovers. Plant in the autumn or spring. Keep well watered until well established.

Maintenance There is little work required during the growing season. They do not usually require staking. Remove dead flowers regularly and tidy up in the autumn. A winter mulch of well-rotted compost is beneficial.

Propagation Lift and divide in October or March. Retain strong outer portions and replant immediately, having first incorporated well-rotted compost if using the same position.

Pests and diseases Ideal plants – generally trouble free.

IRIS

COMMON NAME: FLAGS
FAMILY: IRIDACEAE

This large group of plants is divided into a number of sections. The most widely known are the tall bearded iris, which are at their best in June. There are also dwarf varieties, ideal for the rock garden or front of a border, and intermediates, which usually grow to a height of 60–90cm/24–36in. Among these is the well-known purple or London flag, with rich purple falls, white beard and light purple standards, which flowers in May. Other hardy perennial iris include moisture lovers for alongside a pool or stream. Among these are *Iris sibirica* (AGM), with its numerous varieties, and the later-flowering *Iris ensata* (AGM), which has large flamboyant blooms. Among the marginal iris is *Iris pseudacorous* (AGM), widely known as yellow flag. There are many more.

Iris 'Bandera Waltz'; this variety has lavender standards and purple-edged falls

SPECIES AND VARIETIES The tall bearded iris are those above 70cm/27in in height. They are the last of the bearded group to flower, and at their finest in June – the dwarf varieties mostly flower in April. With a kaleidoscope of colours the choice is enormous, so much so it is very much a matter of personal taste, so I have mentioned only a few. If you are looking for a nearly black iris then 'Black Swan' is well worth considering. Another very attractive iris is 'Wabash', with its white standards and white-edged, bright purple falls. 'Party Dress' is eye-catching, a soft pink with a tangerine beard. The best way to make a selection, with the range available and newcomers constantly added to the formidable lists, is to see them in flower or to obtain a catalogue from an iris specialist. *Iris sibirica* (AGM), Siberian iris, are useful for planting alongside a stream or pond where, left undisturbed, they will produce a sizable clump of grassy foliage. They are also happy in the border in moist soils. Long lived, they will even tolerate neglect. The majority have flowers in shades of blue through to violet, and there are also very attractive white-flowered and pink-flowered varieties. These iris are available in a range of heights from 60cm/24in to 1.2m/4ft. Some that have been around for a great many years are still as popular as ever. Two which are widely available are the early-flowering 'White Swirl' (AGM), a pure white with light gold standards, and the dark blue 'Caesar'.

Iris 'Pink Taffeta'; tall bearded iris are available with blooms of pastel shades and stronger colours

Iris 'Lady Friend'; this border iris and others of the type require an open, sunny position

CULTIVATION

Soil type The tall bearded iris will grow well in most soils but do best in neutral conditions. Before planting, incorporate well-rotted compost or manure and a sprinkling of bone meal. The Siberian iris grow well in good, humus-rich, moist soils.

Planting The tall bearded iris require their rhizomes to receive as much sun as possible – these should just show above the surface. Ensure that they are firmly planted, ideally in midsummer, as this enables them to become well established and to flower the following year. They can also be planted in the spring but may well not flower in the same year.

The best time to plant the Siberians, moisture lovers, is in the spring, in a shallow depression; this depression will help with watering in dry weather and will eventually fill in with soil to the correct level. Again, the plants may not flower in the same year. If planting near water choose a spot 15cm/6in above water level.

Maintenance Throughout the season there is little work required. Both types have strong stems and will not need support. Regular deadheading, especially in the case of the bearded, will greatly improve appearance.

Propagation Lift and divide the bearded iris straight after flowering. Cut the rhizomes and ensure that each portion has two strong fans. Discard the old centre section and replant immediately having first rejuvenated the soil. Spread out the roots and position the rhizomes so that they receive maximum sun. Trimming the leaves by half will help to prevent them being rocked by wind until well established. Most bearded iris require dividing every three to five years. The Siberians should be divided in the autumn after the foliage has died back, or in April just as new growth is starting. Established clumps will usually result in up to eight divisions. Resist the temptation to divide too small, as if a portion does not have enough rhizomes, the plants will take time to build up to flowering size. Plant with the rhizomes 2.5cm/1in below soil level, having first incorporated well-rotted compost.

Pests and diseases There are a number of viral and fungal diseases which can affect iris. While there is no cure for viral diseases, fungal attacks can be controlled with fungicide. In most cases iris are trouble free.

KNIPHOFIA

COMMON NAME: RED HOT POKER
FAMILY: ASPHODELACEAE

No matter what size the garden, there are sun-loving kniphofias to suit, with varieties growing up to 2m/6½ft in height and needing plenty of space. They are superb architectural plants in the right setting. At the other end of the scale are the dwarf varieties, ideal for the smaller garden, with some not exceeding 50cm/20in in height.

Kniphofias originate from South Africa, but are no strangers to British gardens having been grown here for a great many years. Among the taller kniphofias are 'Fiery Fred' with, as its name implies, orange red flowers reaching 90cm/36in in height. Much taller is 'Samuel's Sensation' (AGM), with scarlet red flower spikes in late summer. 'Percy's Pride', reaching 1m/3ft easily in ideal conditions, has sulphur yellow flowers. Among the last to flower is *Kniphofia caulescens*, which has glaucous, wide foliage. The strong, 1.2m/4ft flower spikes, with their distinctive yellow, red-tipped flowers, are at their best in September and October. The dwarf varieties have a charm all of their own. Two from which to choose are 'Candlelight', with its grassy foliage and pure yellow flowers, and 'Little Maid' (AGM), which has similar leaves, but with flowers of ivory white. Both grow to just 60cm/24in in height.

Kniphofia 'Atlanta'; early-flowering, it forms a dense clump with orange red pokers

Kniphofia 'Candlelight'; one of the low-growing varieties suitable for smaller gardens

CULTIVATION

Soil type Most fertile, moisture-retentive soils; must be well drained, especially during winter. They will not tolerate cold, heavy, wet conditions.

Planting This can be done in the autumn but is best done in the spring. Make a hole large enough, spread the roots out and ensure that they have an adequate amount of moisture until well established. They should be left undisturbed for several years to build up a sizable clump. In their first season, a mulch of peat is beneficial to conserve moisture.

Maintenance Deadhead regularly. In cold districts the fleshy crowns should be protected from frost with straw and bracken. In late autumn the remaining foliage should be tied up over the crown to protect it from excessive moisture.

Propagation The usual method is by lifting in the spring and dividing, then replanting immediately, ideally in a fresh location. Kniphofias can also be grown from seed sown in April. Grow on in a nursery bed and plant into flowering positions in the following spring.

Pests and diseases Kniphofias can be attacked by a fungal root rot – if seen treat with fungicide immediately.

LAMIUM

COMMON NAME: DEAD-NETTLE
FAMILY: LAMIACEAE

Lamium maculatum; the dead-nettles, with their speckled leaves, are good ground cover plants

Lamium 'White Nancy' (AGM); silvered foliage and pure white flowers make this ideal for a border front

These are useful hardy perennials for ground cover, successful even in lightly shaded spots. The most widely grown are varieties of *Lamium maculatum* which are also good subjects for edging a path or border.

SPECIES AND VARIETIES Among the numerous varieties available is 'Beacon Silver', with silvery foliage and bright, deep pink flowers. 'White Nancy' (AGM) has similar foliage with, as its name implies, white flowers. 'Roseum' is another good choice as is 'Aureum', which has lovely golden foliage and pink flowers. It requires a cool, moist, lightly shaded spot.

CULTIVATION **Soil type** With the exception of 'Aureum', all the varieties mentioned will grow happily in ordinary garden soils.

Planting This can be done in the autumn or spring. If in spring, ensure a plentiful supply of moisture until they become established.

Maintenance Many lamiums have a rather straggly habit which is easily controlled. After flowering trim over: this will encourage new growth and keep the plant neat.

Propagation Lift and divide established clumps. This can be done in the autumn or spring. Replant immediately.

Pests and diseases In some gardens mildew can become a problem. Spray with a suitable fungicide.

LIATRIS

COMMON NAMES: BLAZING STAR, GAY FEATHERS
FAMILY: ASTERACEAE

These colourful, sun-loving, hardy herbaceous plants are easily grown in most light soils. Heavy, wet conditions can lead to their demise in winter.

SPECIES AND VARIETIES   *Liatris spicata* (syn. *L. callilepsis*), the one most likely to be encountered, is a native of the United States, introduced to Britain well over 200 years ago. Its bright, lilac purple flowers, produced in the summer months, are held on strong 60cm/24in stems. There is also a white form listed simply as 'Alba'.

Liatris 'Kobold'; its spikes of mauve pink, from early summer, are unusual in that they open from the tip first

Another good choice is 'Floristan Weiss'. Always sure to attract attention is 'Kobold' ('Gnome'), which has much shorter spikes, reaching just 40cm/16in and with eye-catching mauve pink flower heads which, in many ways, resemble bottle brushes. It is unusual in that the flowers at the top of the spike open first.

CULTIVATION

Soil type Liatris are best grown in humus-rich, light soils.

Planting Liatris can be planted in the autumn or spring. Keep well watered until established.

Maintenance Regular lifting and dividing every three or four years will keep the plants healthy. Liatris are fairly shallow-rooting; mark the position so that damage is not caused when working on the border before completing the winter clear up.

Propagation Lift and divide the clumps in the spring, retain strong outer portions, replant immediately.

Pests and diseases New growth emerging in the spring can attract slugs, otherwise usually trouble free.

LIRIOPE

COMMON NAME: LILYTURF
FAMILY: CONVALLARIACEAE

Hardy perennial plants which come into bloom in late summer and go on into November are always welcome in the garden, especially as few fit into this category. *Liriope muscari* does just that and has the added bonus of producing a sizable clump of deep green, evergreen, arching, glossy, strap-like foliage – excellent ground cover. The liriope is a native of eastern Asia. It has become popular in recent years and, as a result, a number of very attractive named forms are available, some originating from the United States.

Liriope muscari (AGM); these evergreen perennials, which flower in the autumn, are able to withstand dry conditions

SPECIES AND VARIETIES

Over the years *Liriope muscari* (AGM) has been listed under several names, one of these being *Ophiopogon muscari*. The mauve lilac, long-lasting flowers are reminiscent of grape hyacinths – they are bell-shaped and produced along the length of the 24cm/9½in stem. There are several forms available including 'Lilac Beauty', with lilac flowers held well clear of the foliage, and 'Majestic' which has deeper lilac flowers and dark green leaves. One of the best white-flowered varieties is 'Monroe White'. There are also a number with variegated foliage, of which 'Variegata' is a good choice, having striped cream and green leaves and lilac flowers. *Liriope spicata*, a native of China, has foliage very similar to that of 'Variegata' with the exception of being narrower. The flowers are bright lilac mauve and held on slightly taller stems. It also comes into flower in early autumn and is long lasting. There is a white form listed simply as 'Alba', and a good variegated, 'Silver Dragon', which is best grown in a lightly shaded spot.

CULTIVATION

Soil type They will grow happily in most light soils. Cold, heavy or waterlogged soils are not suitable. These plants have a high drought resistance as their roots have numerous small tubers.

Planting Choose an open, sunny spot: while they will grow in shade, they will not flower as freely in these conditions. Left alone for several years, they will produce a sizable clump without showing any signs of deterioration.

Maintenance Plants can be tidied up in the spring by cutting back the foliage; this must be done before new growth starts. If outgrowing their position, they are not difficult to keep in bounds by simply lifting and dividing.

Propagation Lift the clumps in March or April and divide. Rejuvenate the soil with well-rotted compost unless growing in a new spot.

Pests and diseases New growth can be prone to attack by slugs, especially during the spring.

LUPINUS

COMMON NAME: LUPIN
FAMILY: PAPILLIONACEAE

Attention was drawn to these very colourful plants with the introduction of the Russell Lupins in the 1930s. Lupins are available in a wide range of colours and are easily grown, although only short lived. They need replacing every few years.

SPECIES AND VARIETIES

The modern, large-flowered lupins are descended from the blue-flowered *Lupinus polyphyllus*, a native of North America. The resultant hybrids available in self- and multicolours are very popular for the border, growing to a height of 90–120cm/36–47in. They are at their best in early summer.

Lupinus; not long lived, these are very attractive plants with their tall flower spikes

CULTIVATION

Soil type Lupins grow best in light, neutral, deeply cultivated conditions. Over-rich soils will result in soft growth, which normally requires the plants to be supported.

Planting These are sun lovers but will also succeed in light shade. They can be planted into their flowering positions in the autumn. Be careful with positioning as they resent disturbance.

Maintenance During the summer months, support as required. Regular deadheading is important as it will prevent unwanted seedings and extend the flowering period. Cut down old flowering stems in the late autumn.

Propagation Seed is the best method of increasing stock. Sow in trays of John Innes seed compost in March. Prick out into small pots when large enough to handle and plant into their flowering positions in the autumn. Named varieties and others can be increased by basal cuttings taken in the spring. Root under glass in an equal peat/sand mix. Grow on and, as with seed-raised plants, set into their permanent positions in the autumn.

Pests and diseases Lupins can be attacked by viral and fungal diseases; fungal diseases can be controlled with a fungicide. There is also a grey aphid which can cause problems – if seen spray immediately with a good insecticide.

LYCHNIS

COMMON NAME: CAMPION
FAMILY: CARYOPHYLLACEAE

One plant, a great favourite for cottage gardens, is the magenta *Lychnis coronaria*, a short-lived perennial which will self-sow. Another which will certainly stand out in the border is the vermillion *L. chalcedonica* (AGM), which many will know by its common name, the Maltese cross. Both species were introduced to our gardens in the late sixteenth century.

Lychnis chalcedonica (AGM); the Maltese cross, a sun lover with brilliant vermilion flowers

SPECIES AND VARIETIES

Lychnis chalcedonica (AGM), a native of east Russia and a sun lover, acquired its common name from the shape of its flowers. It grows to 90cm/36in, with flat heads of intense vermilion red flowers from June onwards. There are also white and rose forms. *Lychnis coronaria* is recognizable when not in flower from its woolly, silvery foliage. There are several colours available. It is the single-flowered, crimson magenta which is the best known. The pure white, listed simply as 'Alba' (AGM), has become very popular and, as a result, is widely available. 'Oculata' is another white-flowered variety, this time with a distinctive red eye.

CULTIVATION

Soil type Most well drained, fertile soils.

Planting Lychnis will grow happily in full sun or light shade. Planting can be done either in the autumn or spring.

Maintenance In exposed spots it is likely that these plants will need support in the form of twiggy sticks. Deadhead regularly as *L. coronaria* self-seeds freely. Unwanted plants can simply be removed or given to friends. Tidy in the autumn and cut back any dead stems.

Propagation There are three methods of increasing stock: by seed sown in the spring in a garden frame, by division in early spring, retaining strong portions, and by basal root cuttings taken in the spring, rooting in a frame and growing on to plant out in the autumn.

Pests and diseases Usually little or no problems. *Lychnis chalcedonica* can be affected by a viral disease which mottles the foliage; if seen, destroy the plants.

LYSICHITON

COMMON NAME: SKUNK CABBAGE
FAMILY: ARACEAE

The moisture-loving lysichitons are hardy herbaceous perennials, ideal for growing at the edge of a stream or pond. There are two species available. The spathes are very attractive in the spring. It should be remembered that these are followed by huge leaves which can easily be up to 90cm/36in in length, so their position in the garden should be chosen with care.

Lysichiton americanus (AGM); a moisture lover, the pure yellow spathes appear in the spring, followed by huge foliage

SPECIES AND VARIETIES

Lysichiton americanus (AGM) is a deep-rooting plant with spectacular yellow arum-like spathes and prominent green spadix in March and April. These produce a rather unpleasant scent, hence its common name of skunk cabbage. At this stage the foliage is small and just developing; the huge, glossy leaves grow rapidly as the spathes gradually fade and turn green. As its name indicates, *L. americanus* originates from North America. *Lysichiton camtschatensis* (AGM) is smaller with less glossy foliage and sweetly scented, pure white spathes in early spring. This is an Asiatic plant, equally desirable and requiring the same general conditions.

CULTIVATION

Soil type These plants require deep, humus-rich soil with a plentiful supply of moisture at all times.

Planting The rootstock of lysichitons is easily damaged. This can, in turn, lead to the loss of the plant, so care should be taken when planting out in the spring and once planted, leave undisturbed. Lysichitons will grow well in sun or light shade.

Maintenance There is nothing to do except tidy up in the autumn.

Propagation Lysichitons resent root disturbance. They can be increased by carefully removing the offsets which are produced around the base of old rhizomes. Pot up in a loam-based compost, keep shaded and well watered, and plant out in the following spring. Seed is another method of increasing stock, albeit slow. Sow in a tray of John Innes seed compost and stand this in a tray of shallow water to keep the compost saturated. Prick out into pots and grow on. It is usually two or three years before they are ready for their permanent positions and even longer before spathes are produced.

Pests and diseases They are usually trouble free.

LYSIMACHIA

COMMON NAME: LOOSESTRIFE
FAMILY: PRIMULACEAE

Lysimachia punctata verticillata; a vigorous plant which can be invasive, with spikes of brassy yellow flowers in summer

These are hardy perennials for which a spot should be chosen with care. They can be invasive, especially in moist soils which they love. In the right position they are splendid, very colourful plants.

SPECIES AND VARIETIES

Lysimachia punctata is a native of south-eastern Europe, first introduced to Britain at the start of the nineteenth century. It is a vigorous plant, sometimes seen growing in the wild, producing spikes of brassy yellow flowers on 90cm/36in stems in the summer. *Lysimachia clethroides* (AGM), a native of China and Japan, flowers from late summer onwards, producing a mass of short, arching, terminal white spikes. It soon grows into a sizable plant of 1.2m/4ft – it also has an invasive habit, spreading by creeping roots. There is another popular and well-known member of this family, *L. nummularia* (creeping jenny), a creeping plant often used for growing alongside ponds. It is equally at home in drier conditions, covering itself with bright yellow flowers in the summer. The golden leaved form 'Aurea' (AGM), while very attractive in its own right, is generally not so free-flowering.

CULTIVATION

Soil type Most well drained, moist garden soils.

Planting Lysimachias are equally at home in full sun or lightly shaded spots. Planting can be done anytime between October and March, provided soil and weather conditions are suitable.

Maintenance Only in exposed conditions are the taller lysimachias liable to need support. Remove dead flower spikes regularly. In late autumn cut back and tidy the site.

Propagation Increasing stock is simply a matter of lifting and dividing. Select vigorous outer portions and replant immediately.

Pests and diseases Generally no problems.

LYTHRUM

COMMON NAME: PURPLE LOOSESTRIFE
FAMILY: LYTHRACEAE

Lythrum are moisture lovers which will grow happily in good, moisture-retentive soil, either in sun or light shade. Easily grown and very adaptable, they will even tolerate boggy conditions. *Lythrum salicaria* is a native plant; its reddish purple flower spikes brighten up the banks of streams and ponds.

SPECIES AND VARIETIES

Lythrum salicaria is widely available. There are also many named varieties, one of the best being 'Firecandle' (AGM), or more correctly, 'Feuerkerze', with 1.2m/4ft spikes of rosy red flowers. 'The Beacon' is another good choice, with flowers very similar in colour. 'Robert' is a sturdy variety with blooms of clear pink. Another excellent one not to overlook, of the same colour, is 'Morden's Pink'. One more to consider, which is widely available, is the light pink 'Blush'.

CULTIVATION

Soil type Most humus-rich, moisture-retentive soils.

Planting As with many other hardy perennials, planting can be done in the autumn or spring.

Maintenance There is little work required during the growing and flowering season as lythrum do not require support. Regular deadheading is beneficial and will also help to prevent self-seeding. In the autumn, cut down old stems and tidy up.

Propagation Lythrum are easily increased by division in the autumn or spring. Basal cuttings can also be taken in April. Root in the usual way in a peat/sand mixture.

Pests and diseases These are ideal plants for the border as they are generally trouble free.

Lythrum salicaria 'The Beacon'; a rosy red variety of loosestrife

NEPETA

COMMON NAME: CATMINT
FAMILY: LAMIACEAE

The sun-loving, ground-covering, free-flowering catmint, with its aromatic foliage so loved by cats (who enjoy rolling about on the plants, much to the annoyance of gardeners), is a real old stager which has been with us for over 200 years. Many cottage gardens have nepeta as an edging plant.

Nepeta 'Dropmore Blue'; a superb edging plant – sure to find favour with cats, who love to roll in it

SPECIES AND VARIETIES *Nepeta* x *faassenii* is of garden origin and often seen listed as *N. mussinii*. It is a bushy plant with small grey green leaves. The 15cm/6in spikes of lavender blue flowers first appear in June, usually continuing into early autumn, especially if old flower stems are cut back after the main flush is over. Much larger is the variety 'Six Hills Giant' which grows to 60cm/24in and is probably a hybrid. This free-flowering plant is superb when grown in association with roses and hardy geraniums. There are varieties smaller in stature, others with white flowers, and also variegated foliage.

CULTIVATION **Soil type** Most well drained garden soils in full sun or light shade.

Planting This can be done in the autumn or spring.

Maintenance Trimming back after the first flush of flowers will ensure a longer display. Tidy up in the autumn.

Propagation The best method is by division in the spring, ensuring that they do not dry out until well established.

Pests and diseases Powdery mildew can be a problem and should be sprayed with fungicide, otherwise trouble free.

OENOTHERA

COMMON NAME: EVENING PRIMROSE
FAMILY: ONAGRACEAE

The brilliant sun-loving oenotheras, with their long flowering period, are not seen as often in our gardens as they justly deserve. Easily grown in well drained soils, they will certainly brighten up the border.

Oenothera 'Fyrverkeri' (AGM), often listed as 'Fireworks'; this produces cup-shaped, brilliant yellow flowers over a long period

SPECIES AND VARIETIES

Oenothera macrocarpa (AGM) will probably be known to many gardeners by its former name, *O. missouriensis*. This plant produces large, light yellow flowers of 7–10cm/3–4in across, for several weeks. It has a low-growing habit, just 10cm/4in in height. The flowers are followed by sizable seed pods. It is also useful for a sunny open pocket on the rock garden.

The taller growing *O. fruticosa* 'Fyrverkeri' (AGM), sometimes listed as 'Fireworks', is a first class member of the family. Growing to 35cm/14in, it produces sprays of bright yellow, cup-shaped blooms over multicoloured foliage. Flowering commences in June and goes on until late summer. *Oenothera fruticosa* var. *riparia* is normally around 30cm/12in, also with bright yellow flowers.

CULTIVATION

Soil type Oenotheras are best in light, well drained soil.

Planting Planting can be done either in the autumn or spring. Choose an open, sunny site.

Maintenance In dry weather water well. Cut down to ground level in the

Oenothera macrocarpa, formerly known as *O. missouriensis*; a low-growing plant with some of the largest flowers of this genus

autumn and tidy the border. Oenotheras are not particularly long lived. Many will self-seed.

Propagation The species can be raised from seed sown in the spring. When large enough to handle, prick out into nursery rows or small pots and grow on. Plant into their permanent positions in the autumn. The named varieties do not come true from seed. Lift in early spring and carefully divide the roots. Select strong outer portions and replant immediately.

Pests and diseases Powdery mildew can be a problem, spray with a good fungicide as soon as seen.

PAEONIA

COMMON NAME: PEONY
FAMILY: PAEONIACEAE

The flamboyant peonies are certainly among the most handsome plants for the border. Long lived, once planted leave undisturbed and they will steadily build up into sizable clumps. The cardinal red *Paeonia officinalis* 'Rubra Plena' (AGM) has been grown in our gardens for a great many years. Some of those listed today are real old stagers: 'Duchesse de Nemours' (AGM) goes back to 1856, and 'Festiva Maxima' (AGM) was introduced five years before that. Both are still very popular and are obtainable from many sources.

SPECIES AND VARIETIES

One of the earliest to flower is the primrose yellow *Paeonia mlokosewitschii* (AGM), often referred to as Molly the witch. It was discovered in the Caucasus in 1900. In time it builds up into a sizable plant and normally comes into flower in mid-spring. *Paeonia officinalis* has been grown for hundreds of years. The double 'Rubra Plena' and pink-flowered 'Rosea Plena' and 'Anemoniflora Rosea', all AGM holders, are widely known. There are also a number of others including the white 'Alba Plena' and *P. peregrina*, another with a history going back a great many years. Known as the red peony of Constantinople, it has also been referred to by a number of species names. Its brilliant, ruby red flowers are held on 50cm/20in stems over shiny, dark green foliage. There are many more species. *Paeonia lactiflora* (Chinese paeony) is still available commercially but is not often seen. Today it is the host of garden forms and hybrids which provide so much colour, as they have done for many years. These wonderful plants are available with single, semi-double and fully-double blooms in a wide range of colours. The earliest originates from France, with others coming from Kelways of Langport, Somerset, who supply a very comprehensive range. In more recent times numerous varieties have been introduced from America. One which caused quite a stir on its debut in 1949 is 'Bowl of Beauty' (AGM). It is still very popular today, hence its wide availability. A lovely rich pink with a centre of pale cream staminodes, it is a mid-season variety and grows to 90cm/36in. There is a whole host of others from which to choose, including 'Bunker Hill', a cherry red semi-double with golden yellow stamens, and the much more recent 'Top Brass', an ivory white with petaloids of a very similar colour, and a centre tuft of pink petals.

CULTIVATION

Soil type Most humus-rich, well drained soils are suitable. Dig the ground at least one spit deep and incorporate well-rotted manure and compost: this will feed the plants and help to retain moisture. Avoid cold, waterlogged soils.

Paeonia mlokosewitschii (AGM); early-flowering and widely known as Molly the witch

Paeonia 'Bowl of Beauty' (AGM); one of the most popular peonies and widely available

Paeonia officinalis 'Anemoniflora Rosea' (AGM); a low-growing variety which slowly produces a sizable clump

Planting This can either be in the autumn or spring. It is most important to plant at the correct depth, too deep and the plants may fail to flower. The crowns should be no more than 2.5cm/1in below the surface. Water spring plantings in dry weather.

Maintenance Mulch with well-rotted manure or compost in the spring. Ensure a plentiful supply of moisture during the summer months. Some of the taller varieties may need support – use twiggy sticks for this as they are not so obtrusive. Remove any dead flowers. In the autumn a top dressing of bone meal or low nitrogen fertilizer is beneficial. Once planted, leave undisturbed. If it is necessary to move an established plant, dig round and retain as much soil as possible without disturbing the roots. Peonies can, in some circumstances, take a year or so to settle down after a move.

Propagation Divide established clumps in early autumn. Lift carefully and split the crown into pieces; each section should have four or five buds. It is advisable to dust the roots with fungicide before replanting. After division it is unlikely that the plants will flower for a year or so.

Pests and diseases Peonies are generally problem free. The most troublesome diseases which affect them are the fungal diseases, which can become a nuisance in late season. These should be treated with a fungicide.

PAPAVER

COMMON NAME: ORIENTAL POPPY
FAMILY: PAPAVERACEAE

Oriental poppies, *Papaver orientale*, with their gorgeous flowers, have been grown in this country for around 300 years, since they were introduced from Armenia. During this time many splendid varieties have been introduced, with many of the more recent introductions originating from Germany.

Papaver 'Perry's White'; an old favourite, as popular as ever and widely available

SPECIES AND VARIETIES

Papaver orientale has large, brilliant scarlet flowers with a distinctive black blotch at the base of the petals. It is a fine sight when in flower, but the foliage normally dies away during the summer months, leaving unsightly gaps in the border. This can be overcome by planting *Gypsophila paniculata* behind the poppy; the masses of foliage and flowers soon cover the gap. In the following autumn or spring the poppy will reappear. Over the years there have been many varieties of these very impressive poppies introduced, both singles and semi-doubles, in a range of colours. 'Beauty of Livermere' is a good choice, with its blood red, single flowers. Others to look out for are the glowing, flesh pink 'Turkish Delight', the old stager 'Black and White', 'Picotée', a combination of scarlet and white with frilly edges to the petals, 'Glowing Embers', as its name implies, a glowing orange red with ruffled petals, and 'Patty's Plum', with deep rose blooms. A newcomer which is sure to become popular, from the famous Countess von Zeppelen nursery, is the scarlet 'Blickfang' which, when translated, means 'Arresting Sight'. There are a great many more splendid examples, far too numerous to mention here.

CULTIVATION

Soil type Papaver are easy to grow in most well drained soils.

Planting Planting can be carried out in the autumn or spring in either full sun or light shade.

Maintenance These poppies have a rather sprawling habit and do need supporting. Pea sticks are ideal for this as they are not obtrusive. Regular deadheading is beneficial.

Propagation Lift and divide the clumps in early spring and replant immediately. Any roots left behind will probably grow into new plants. These poppies can also be increased from root cuttings taken during mid-winter and inserted in a garden frame.

Pests and diseases Downy mildew can attack the foliage. If flowering has finished, cut back to within 2cm/¾in of the ground – new growth will soon appear.

Papaver 'Glowing Embers'; an oriental poppy with gorgeous ruffled petals and rich red flowers

PENSTEMON

COMMON NAME: BEARD TONGUE
FAMILY: SCROPHULARIACEAE

These are sun-loving plants which have become very popular in recent years. They are not fully hardy, except in very sheltered positions, but they will come through most winters satisfactorily if given well drained soil and a mulch as protection. As a general rule, the larger the flower and leaves, the more tender the variety.

Penstemon 'Sour Grapes', with a background of kniphofias; introduced in the late 1940s

Penstemon 'Andenken an Friedrich', previously known as 'Garnet'; one of the finest reds

SPECIES AND VARIETIES   The penstemons more commonly seen are hybrids, available in a wide range of colours. One which is a great favourite is 'Andenken an Friedrich' (AGM) sometimes still listed under its old name 'Garnet'. It grows to 50cm/20in and has wine red flowers. Others include 'Sour Grapes', an unusual name for this vigorous variety with pale purple flowers, and 'White Bedder' (AGM), formerly 'Snow Storm', which is a good white. For those who like pink flowers then 'Pink Endurance', with smaller blooms, is a good choice.

CULTIVATION   **Soil type** Penstemons will grow in most ordinary, well drained soils.

Planting This should be done in the spring in an open, sunny position. Avoid positions where they would be subjected to cold, drying winds.

Maintenance There is little required during the summer except to ensure that they do not dry out. Remove any dead flower spikes. In the autumn cut down to just above soil level and protect the crowns with mulch. It is a good idea to take some cuttings in the autumn as a precaution and to overwinter them under glass.

Propagation Take cuttings in late summer/early autumn, selecting non-flowering shoots of around 7cm/3in in length. Root in an equal peat/sand mix and place in a garden frame. They should be well-rooted by the following spring and can then be planted into their flowering positions.

Pests and diseases Normally trouble free. Avoid overfeeding: this will result in lush growth and make the plant more susceptible to pests and diseases. It will also result in poor flowering.

123

PERSICARIA

COMMON NAME: KNOTWEED
FAMILY: POLYGONACAE

Persicaria bistorta 'Superba' (AGM); an excellent, long-flowering moisture lover which is widely available

These are moisture lovers, happy both in full sun and in light shade. Many of the plants which are now included in this genus were formerly listed as polygonums.

SPECIES AND VARIETIES
Persicaria amplexicaulis is a vigorous plant producing considerable quantities of small, heart-shaped leaves which makes it good for ground cover. The long succession of red terminal spikes commence in June and continue through into the autumn. There are a number of named varieties. 'Atrosanguinea' is a good choice, with deep crimson flower spikes of 1m/3ft in height. 'Firetail' (AGM) is an excellent bright red. Another one not to overlook is 'Cottesbrook Gold', its golden foliage a perfect foil for the red flower spikes. 'Inverleith' is a neat plant with masses of dull crimson heads on 60cm/24in stems. Different again is *P. a.* var. *pendula*, with curving, dark pink, bronze-tipped flower heads. Providing contrast is the white form listed simply as 'Alba'. If you are looking for a good bog plant then *Persicaria bistorta* is a splendid choice, especially 'Superba' (AGM), with its rich pink flowers, on display over a long period and held well clear of the lush foliage on wiry 90cm/36in stems. This plant will often flower through until the first sharp autumn frosts. *Persicaria virginiana* and the varieties are grown mainly for their attractive foliage. 'Painter's Palette' has a rich mixture of cream, black and pink. It forms a sizable clump and looks particularly attractive in a lightly shaded border. There are two others well worth growing: 'Lance Corporal', with single black chevrons on the leaves, and 'Compton's Form', with a chevron of olive green.

The latter should be planted in a sheltered, warm spot as it will not survive severe winter conditions. There is another group of persicarias often grown in the rock garden; they are a good ground cover and are certainly not out of place at the front of a border. *Persicaria affinis*, a native of the Himalayas, is a variable plant with white or pink flower heads on 20cm/8in stems. One which has become very popular is 'Darjeeling Red' (AGM), on which the flowers open pink and gradually turn to crimson. 'Donald Lowndes' (AGM) is a pinkish salmon, 'Ron McBeath' a mid-pink with grey green foliage, and the widely available 'Superba' (AGM) has light pink flowers turning to crimson as they age.

CULTIVATION

Soil type Most humus-rich soils, provided they are moisture-retentive, in either sun or light shade.

Planting This can be done in the autumn or spring.

Maintenance Deadheading of the taller varieties will help to extend the display. The old flower spikes of *Persicaria affinis* are attractive during the winter; in other cases tidy up in the autumn.

Propagation Persicaria are easily increased by division which can be done either in the autumn or spring. Select strong outer portions and discard any old, woody centre sections. Replant immediately.

Pests and diseases They are generally without problems.

PHLOX

COMMON NAME: NONE
FAMILY: POLEMONIACEAE

These are free-flowering, useful plants for the border and have been a feature of our gardens for many years. A host of named varieties are available in a wide range of colours.

Phlox 'Fujiyama' (AGM); one of the best whites available

Phlox 'Jules Sandeau'; an old stager with masses of deep pink flowers

SPECIES AND VARIETIES

It is mostly the cultivars of *Phlox paniculata* which are available for the border. They range in height from 30–90cm/12–36in. Several have been awarded the RHS Award of Garden Merit, among them 'Brigadier', a striking orange red, 'Prince of Orange', a salmon orange, 'Bright Eyes', a soft pink with a red eye, and the pure white 'Fujiyama' which is a later flowering variety. There are many more equally desirable. If you are looking for bright red then 'Starfire' is a good choice. 'Prospero', with charming, light lilac flowers, is vigorous and 'Border Gem', a violet purple, is an old stager. Other 'hot' colours are 'Red Indian', a crimson red, and 'Windsor', a glowing carmine with a magenta eye. The varieties with variegated foliage are particularly attractive. 'Norah Leigh', probably the best known, and 'Harlequin' have purple flowers.

CULTIVATION

Soil type Phlox require moisture-retentive, well drained, humus-rich soils in an open, sunny position.

Planting Either in the autumn or early spring.

Maintenance Established plants will benefit from a mulch of well-rotted compost in the spring; this also helps to retain moisture. During hot, dry weather water well. Supporting is not usually necessary unless grown in particularly exposed positions. In this case, supporting with twiggy sticks is usually sufficient. In the autumn cut down old stems and tidy the site.

Propagation Propagation is by division of healthy plants in the autumn or spring. Retain strong outer portions and replant immediately. If eelworm is present (see Pests and diseases, below), root cuttings can be taken in the spring. Root in John Innes seed compost in a cold frame, grow on in nursery rows and plant out in the following spring. New plants can also be increased by stem cuttings taken in the spring. Root in an equal mix of peat and sand, then treat as root cuttings. Only healthy stock should be propagated in this way as eelworms, if present, can be carried over into cuttings. If in doubt, use the root cutting system, which will be free of infestation.

Pests and diseases The major pest to the phlox is the eelworm. Its presence is indicated by the appearance of twisted, distorted stems and leaves. Infected plants should be lifted and burnt. Do not plant phlox in the same spot again as there is a risk of infection. Mildew can cause problems; a free supply of air around the plants can help to prevent this. Slugs and snails will also attack new growth in the spring.

POLEMONIUM

Common name: Jacob's ladder
Family: Polemoniaceae

This family of hardy herbaceous plants includes the old cottage garden favourite *Polemonium caeruleum*, commonly known as Jacob's ladder; its leaves alternate with leaflets in pairs which resemble the rungs of a ladder, no doubt giving rise to this common name. There are other species in cultivation but this is the one that is best known.

Polemonium 'Brise d'Anjou'; this charming, variegated Jacob's ladder was raised in France. It grows best in a cool, lightly shaded spot

Species and varieties	*Polemonium caeruleum*, with saucer-shaped, lavender blue flowers on 60cm/24in stems, is easily grown. There is also a white form, *P. caeruleum* subsp. *caeruleum* f. *album*, which is widely available. One hybrid that has become popular in recent years is the pure white 'Dawn Flight', with flowers held clear of the light green, fern-like foliage. With the interest in variegated foliage plants, the very attractive French-raised 'Brise d'Anjou', introduced a few years ago, was sure of being well received. This graceful plant has finely divided, yellow-edged foliage over which, during June and July, violet blue flowers appear.
Cultivation	**Soil type** Most fertile, well drained garden soils which are moisture-retentive are suitable. 'Brise d'Anjou' prefers a lightly shaded spot with cool, moist conditions that do not dry out.

Planting This can be done in the autumn or spring – planting in spring will enable the plant to grow away quickly. Always ensure a plentiful supply of moisture, especially in hot, dry weather.

Maintenance Polemoniums are short lived. *Polemonium caeruleum* will self-sow. The taller varieties can be damaged by summer storms so support is usually necessary. The fibrous roots quickly exhaust the soil; division every two or three years will keep the plants vigorous and free-flowering. After flowering, cut down the dead stems and tidy up the area.

Propagation Division is the usual method of increasing polemonium stock and can be done in the autumn or spring. Select strong outer portions and replant immediately.

Pests and diseases Mildew can occasionally affect the plants after flowering, in which case cut off affected foliage and burn.

PRIMULA

Common name: Primrose
Family: Primulaceae

This is a large family which includes the well-known primrose and gold-laced polyanthus, and the stately, moisture-loving Asiatic primulas which are ideal for the side of streams or bog gardens.

Primula 'Wisley Red'; ideal for the front of a border

Primula prolifera (AGM); an impressive candelabra primula commonly known as glory of the bog

SPECIES AND VARIETIES

Our native primrose, *P. vulgaris*, is one of our most popular wild flowers. Its cheerful yellow blooms appear in early spring. There are numerous named varieties, many hybrids, ideal for planting in groups or at the front of the border. Among them are 'Guinevere', a soft pink, 'Wanda' (AGM), a bright red, and the white-flowered 'Snowcushion', now more correctly known as 'Schneekissen'. There is also a whole host of double primroses, great favourites in Victorian times and now enjoying a resurgence of interest. These range from the deep purple 'Miss Indigo' to the ruby red 'Red Velvet'. Also very popular are the gold-laced polyanthus. The best known of the Asiatic primulas is *P. denticulata* (AGM). Once only available in lavender shades, there are now reds, ruby and pure white. *Primula denticulata* is known as the drumstick primula as it has a rounded head of tightly packed flowers. *Primula vialii* (AGM) is a very distinctive species with tight, pointed heads, in many ways resembling a red hot poker. The flowers at the bottom are lavender, the buds are scarlet. There are several varieties which come within the Candelabra Group. *Primula pulverulenta* (AGM) is well known, with rich crimson purple flowers. *Primula japonica* (AGM) is more widely represented by two forms, both with self-explanatory names, 'Miller's Crimson' and 'Posford White'. One of the finest sights alongside a stream or pond has to be a group of *Primula prolifera* (AGM), with its rich golden yellow flowers on strong stems which eventually reach 1m/3ft in height in ideal conditions. Ideal for the bog garden, moist or wet conditions is the Himalayan cowslip, *P. florindae* (AGM). Its 60cm/24in stems have long-lasting, drooping, fragrant, yellow bell-shaped flowers and large rounded leaves. It is a vigorous plant happy in sun or lightly shaded areas.

CULTIVATION

Soil type Primulas generally enjoy cool, moist, humus-rich soil and one which is not too light. The Asiatic primulas require a moisture-retentive soil; this is especially so in the case of *P. florindae*.

Planting This can be done either in autumn or spring, in full sun or light shade, and in moist conditions.

Maintenance Deadhead on a regular basis. The taller varieties will welcome a top dressing of well-rotted compost in the spring.

Propagation All of those mentioned can be increased by division in early spring. The species can also be raised from seed. This should be sown as soon as ripe in John Innes seed compost. Prick out into small pots when the seedlings are large enough to handle and grow on until ready for planting into their permanent positions.

Pests and diseases The worst pest to attack primulas is the vine weevil. The adult damages the edges of the foliage, but it is the white grubs which cause the most problems by attacking the roots. Often nothing is suspected until the plant collapses and can be lifted off. The best method of treatment is to use the harmless parasitic nematodes now offered by several companies. The soil temperature must be high enough for the nematodes to work satisfactorily. Applications in early summer and autumn are usually sufficient.

There are a small number of viral and fungal diseases which can also cause problems. It is best to lift and destroy any plants affected by a virus; fungal attacks can be treated with fungicide.

PULMONARIA

COMMON NAME: LUNGWORT
FAMILY: BORAGINACEAE

Pulmonaria 'Lewis Palmer', formerly and still occasionally seen under its old name 'Highdown'

Among the first hardy perennials to flower are pulmonarias – best known by their common name lungwort – usually at their best in March. They associate well with hellebores and daffodils. These plants are native to Europe and occur over a vast area. They are mostly found at higher altitudes, enjoying cool, moist conditions, although they can be seen at lower levels too. Pulmonarias should be grown where they are protected from hot sun, ideally among deciduous shrubs. If in a

Pulmonaria; these plants bloom early in the year when their flowers are particularly welcome

border, choose a spot where they will have some shade from taller subjects during the summer months. These very free-flowering plants thrive in cool, moist, humus-rich conditions. They will not succeed in waterlogged areas and are not successful in extremely dry, poor, sandy soils. Mulching with leaf mould or well-rotted compost in the summer is beneficial and helps to keep the thick, fleshy rhizomes cool.

There are 18 species and a legion of named varieties of these very desirable plants; this leads to some confusion, not helped by the fact that pulmonarias hybridize readily. Frequently, seedlings occur in an established clump and are all too easily wrongly named before distribution. Pulmonarias are readily available with blue, violet, red, pink and white flowers. Many are also noted for their attractive foliage, which may be heavily spotted, silvery, or blotched. The leaves and stems are hairy and in some cases quite rough to touch. Grown in our gardens for a great many years, their common name, lungwort, is thought to date back to a seventeenth-century medical theory, the spotted leaves resembling diseased lungs. There are several other cultivars associated with various species of pulmonaria, one example being *P. officinalis* 'Soldiers and Sailors', whose flowers change from pink to violet blue with age.

SPECIES AND VARIETIES   *Pulmonaria angustifolia* is native to central Europe. It is a good ground cover plant with plain green foliage, producing sizable clumps, and dies down for the winter. There are a number of named cultivars including one which has been around for over 60 years, 'Mawson's Variety'. *Pulmonaria longifolia* is widely distributed in western Europe and can be found in Britain. This has long, narrow, dark green leaves with bright silvery markings. It is more tolerant of sunnier and drier positions in the garden. *Pulmonaria officinalis* has been grown in English gardens for over 400 years and has become naturalized in some areas. It is another with spotted foliage and is well known both for its free-flowering habit and its flower colour – pink initially, changing to violet blue with age. *Pulmonaria rubra* is the first to flower – as early as December in suitable conditions. The leaves are thin and long, reaching up to 30cm/12in. The lovely bell-shaped, pink flowers are particularly welcome early in the season. A vigorous plant, ideal among shrubs, it will quickly show if it is short of moisture by flagging quite dramatically; given a good watering it is usually back to normal overnight. The foliage of *Pulmonaria saccharata* can be spotted or an overall silvery grey, bristly to the touch. All those mentioned are readily obtainable. Only a few named varieties can be mentioned here, each year seeing the list of those available increasing. One old favourite is 'Sissinghurst White' (AGM) which is widely available. Another, sure to catch one's eye, is the bright 'Blue Ensign' (AGM). The blue-flowered 'Lewis Palmer' (AGM) was for years listed as 'Highdown'. 'Leopard' (AGM) has reddish pink flowers held on short stems over spotted foliage. Any which are listed simply as the Cambridge Blue Group are usually a good choice, if something of a lucky dip. Most have light blue flowers and spotted leaves.

CULTIVATION

Soil type Humus-rich and moisture-retentive are two of the most important soil characteristics to grow pulmonarias successfully. If these are present, they will grow in most conditions, with the exception of waterlogged soils.

Planting This can be done in the autumn or spring, ideally in a lightly shaded spot in soil prepared by the addition of well-rotted compost, leaf mould and a good general fertilizer. Established plants will benefit from a top dressing in the autumn and mulching during the summer to help keep the soil cool and moist. Water well in hot, dry conditions. Pulmonarias can be left undisturbed for three or four years; after this they tend to deteriorate in the centre of the clump and should be lifted and divided.

Maintenance Remove dead flower heads regularly. Old foliage can be removed in the winter, prior to new growth starting.

Propagation The best and easiest method of increasing stock is by division in the autumn or spring. Carefully lift and divide the clumps, discard old woody rhizomes but retain strong outer sections with good root growth. Replant as soon as possible, ideally in a fresh spot; if not, rejuvenate the soil beforehand. Pulmonarias can be easily raised from seed which is best sown as soon as ripe. The species interbreed freely and are unlikely to be true, especially if other pulmonarias are grown nearby.

Pests and diseases Many pulmonarias are affected by powdery mildew in the summer, especially in dry conditions. Fungicides can be used as treatment on these plants but mildew can be very difficult to control. Slugs and snails can be a nuisance, attacking foliage, otherwise they are generally trouble free.

RHEUM

COMMON NAME: ORNAMENTAL RHUBARB
FAMILY: POLYGONACEAE

Of the two species that are widely grown as ornamental plants, it is *Rheum palmatum* which is the most often seen. It is a handsome, moisture-loving plant with large, jagged-edged, rounded leaves. As it forms a sizable clump, it should be given plenty of space. One of the best positions for it is alongside a stream or pond in a lightly shaded area. This rheum is no stranger to our gardens, being introduced from China in the mid-eighteenth century.

Rheum alexandrae; not the easiest plant to grow, it has large cream bracts which become tinged with red as they age

SPECIES AND VARIETIES   The most spectacular variety of *Rheum palmatum* is 'Atrosanguineum'. The young growth in spring is a vivid red, a colour which is retained on the back of the leaves until flowering time, while the top slowly changes to green. In early summer the flowering spikes appear. These reach 1.8m/6ft in height and are topped with large, fluffy panicles of bright red flowers – a splendid architectural plant which is sure to attract attention. There are a number of other named varieties available: 'Bowles' Crimson', as its name implies, is a wonderful crimson red variety. Do not overlook *Rheum palmatum* (AGM) itself. It forms a lovely specimen plant, again with red flowers. *Rheum alexandrae* is a native of the Himalayas, not as often seen in our gardens as it seems to miss the cool mountain climate. However, when grown well it is a very distinctive plant, with plain green, shiny foliage. In early summer it produces 90cm/36in stems with cream bracts along the length; as these age they take on a reddish tint. Positioning is a key to success – it requires a cool, moist, lightly shaded spot.

CULTIVATION

Soil type Deeply cultivated, humus-rich, moist soil.

Planting Dig over and incorporate well-rotted compost into the chosen site. Planting can be done in suitable soil conditions between November and February. Some rheums can be damaged by sun scorch on the leaves; choose a lightly shaded position. Once planted they can be left undisturbed for several years, until it becomes necessary to lift and divide.

Maintenance There is little to do during the growing season. Ensure a plentiful supply of water during hot, dry weather. Rheums will benefit from an occasional application of liquid fertilizer up to flowering time. Cut down old flowering stems. In the autumn tidy the site.

Propagation Carefully lift the crowns between November and February while plants are dormant. Divide, checking that each section has a dormant bud. Rheum can also be raised from seed. Sow in the spring and when large enough to handle, prick out into a nursery bed. Grow on, keeping moist during the summer months. By late autumn of the following year they should be large enough to plant into their flowering positions.

Pests and diseases These are ideal garden subjects as they are generally trouble free.

RUDBECKIA

COMMON NAME: CONEFLOWER
FAMILY: ASTERACEAE

Hardy perennial plants which will flower well into autumn – often until brought to an abrupt end by the first sharp frosts – are particularly welcome. One which can be relied upon to do just that is *Rudbeckia fulgida* 'Goldsturm' (AGM).

SPECIES AND VARIETIES

Rudbeckia fulgida var. *deamii* (AGM) is a very popular plant, producing yellow flowers with prominent black centres on 75cm/30in stems. 'Goldsturm' was raised in Germany in 1937, a slightly taller variety with masses of bright yellow flowers, again with a black centre cone up to 12cm/5in across. Other popular varieties are 'Goldquelle' (AGM), with fully double, chrome yellow flowers on strong 1m/3ft stems over mid-green foliage. 'Herbstonne', sometimes offered as 'Autumn Sun', is much taller, usually reaching 2.1m/7ft in height. It has large, single yellow flowers with a prominent green central boss. This is a useful plant for the back of the border. Flowering starts in August and continues until early autumn.

CULTIVATION

Soil type Rudbeckias are easily grown in most fertile, well drained soils which never dry out, ideally in a lightly shaded spot, though they will grow satisfactorily in full sun provided they are not short of moisture. 'Goldsturm' is

Rudbeckia 'Goldsturm'; a splendid plant for a late show, usually going on to the first sharp autumn frosts. Introduced in 1937

a splendid plant for growing at the side of a pool where it can enjoy cool, moist conditions.

Planting Ideally they should be planted in the spring, ensuring a plentiful supply of water until well established. Mulching with peat or well-rotted compost is beneficial.

Maintenance Regular deadheading will help. Cut back the dead foliage in late autumn and tidy the site.

Propagation Rudbeckias can be carefully lifted and divided in the autumn or spring. Select strong outer portions and replant immediately.

Pests and diseases Slugs and snails will attack these plants – take precautions early (see Chapter 5, page 36).

SEDUM

COMMON NAME: STONECROP
FAMILY: CRASSULACEAE

This large family contains many hardy perennials, splendid subjects for the border. All are easy to grow, most being sun lovers.

SPECIES AND VARIETIES When many of the border perennials are past their best, *Sedum spectabile* (AGM), often referred to as ice plant, produces its very colourful, flat, mauve pink heads which are made up of hundreds of tiny star-shaped flowers. Not only does it provide a very colourful display, it also attracts butterflies, especially on a warm, sunny, early autumn day. There are a number of named varieties including 'Brilliant' (AGM), a vivid deep rose. Others, of varying shades, are 'Septemberglut' ('September Glow'), 'Indian Chief' and 'Meteor'. There is also a good white 'Iceberg'. The flower heads are held on stout 45cm/18in stems over fleshy, glaucous, grey green foliage. Another good choice is 'Herbstfreude' (AGM), still often listed as 'Autumn Joy'. This is a hybrid with heads of rich pink flowers which, as they age, gradually turn, first to a salmon bronze and eventually to a rich coppery red. For those who enjoy variegated foliage *Sedum alboroseum* 'Mediovariegatum' is a good choice, its foliage heavily marked with creamy yellow. In complete contrast is *Sedum telephium* subsp. *maximum* 'Atropurpureum' (AGM), with rich purple red leaves and, in late summer, heads of rosy red flowers on 50cm/20in stems.

CULTIVATION

Soil type Sedum are happy in ordinary, well drained soils. *Sedum telephium* requires a moisture-retentive soil.

Planting Best planted in the spring as they are commencing growth; if more convenient, they can be planted in the autumn. Most are drought resistant due to their fleshy leaves.

Maintenance Throughout the season sedums require little in the way of attention. It is best to leave the dead flower stems on the plant until early spring when they are easily removed. Some, 'Autumn Joy' is an example, turn a rich brown which adds colour to the winter garden. Lift and divide every two or three years to keep them vigorous.

Propagation These are among the easiest plants to lift and divide: portions with little in the way of roots will usually grow away satisfactorily.

Pests and diseases Although easy to grow, there are a number of pests which can cause problems. By far the most troublesome is vine weevil – the grubs eat away at the roots. If suspected it is best to treat with a natural predator, in this case nematodes. Instructions must be carefully observed as the soil temperature must be correct. Slugs and snails can also attack new growth. In wet conditions fungal diseases can set up crown or root rot, for which there is no cure.

Sedum spectabile 'Brilliant'; at their best in September, these are particularly attractive to butterflies

SISYRINCHIUM

Common name: None
Family: Iridaceae

There are only a small number of these hardy perennials suitable for growing in the border, the majority of them being suitable for the rock garden.

Sisyrinchium striatum; a native of Chile, introduced in the late eighteenth century. Produces slender spikes of pale yellow flowers in early summer

SPECIES AND VARIETIES *Sisyrinchium striatum* originates from the Chilean Andes but is no stranger to our gardens, having been introduced over 200 years ago. This plant produces a clump of iris-like, grey green, evergreen leaves. The flowering stem is 60cm/24in in height with pale yellow flowers along its length during June and July. The variety 'Aunt May', sometimes listed as 'Variegatum', has leaves striped with creamy yellow. 'Aunt May' originated in a garden in Devon. Sisyrinchiums are not long lived, but are prolific self-seeders, and young plants can be lifted and planted elsewhere. Keep a few to replace any sudden losses among mature plants.

CULTIVATION **Soil type** Most humus-rich, well drained soil.

Planting Sisyrinchium are sun lovers. Planting can be done either in the autumn or spring.

Maintenance For best results sisyrinchium should be lifted and divided frequently. If the same spot is used, incorporate plenty of well-rotted compost before replanting: this will keep the plants vigorous and lead to better flowering. They do not require support. Remove dead flower stems regularly to avoid self-seeding. In the autumn tidy up any dead foliage.

Propagation Division in the autumn or spring, or alternatively, by seed sown in a tray of John Innes seed compost and placed in a frame. When the seedlings are large enough to handle, prick out in a nursery bed. Plant into flowering positions in the autumn or spring.

Pests and diseases The grubs of the vine weevil can attack the roots (see Chapter 5, page 37).

SOLIDAGO

COMMON NAME: GOLDEN ROD
FAMILY: ASTERACEAE

These very colourful, hardy herbaceous perennials have rather fallen from favour in recent years, partly due to their susceptibility to mildew late in the season and partly due to their needing support, the older varieties in particular. In spite of this, there are several species and numerous varieties available, ranging from 25cm/10in to almost 2m/6½ft in height.

Solidago 'Golden Shower'; easily grown in most soils, this variety is widely known as 'Golden Rod'

SPECIES AND VARIETIES

One of the smallest is 'Queenie' at just 25cm/10in, with yellow spikes in September/October. Only one member of the family has been awarded the coveted Award of Garden Merit to date – 'Goldenmosa'. This is a neat plant with light green foliage and lovely yellow plumes on 70cm/27in stems, at their best in midsummer.

CULTIVATION

Soil type Ordinary fertile garden soil suits these plants well, either in a sunny or lightly shaded spot.

Planting This can be done in the autumn or spring. Keep well watered in dry weather until established.

Maintenance The taller varieties will almost certainly need support. Cut back as soon as flowering has finished to avoid self-seeding. Some are vigorous and will need to be kept in check. In the autumn, tidy and remove all dead foliage.

Propagation This can be done any time between autumn and spring, in suitable ground and weather conditions. Clumps can be lifted and divided. Replant only strong outer portions.

Pests and diseases Mildew can become a problem late in the season, especially after a long dry period. Treat with fungicide or cut back plants if flowering has finished.

STACHYS

COMMON NAME: LAMB'S TONGUE (*S. BYZANTINA*)
FAMILY: LAMIACEAE

Two species of this large family are popular ground cover plants. The one referred to as lamb's tongue, formerly listed as *Stachys lanata* and now more correctly known as *S. byzantina*, is easily recognized by its soft, downy foliage. *Stachys macrantha,* in contrast, is a very showy, free-flowering plant.

Stachys macrantha 'Violacea'; a showy plant with crinkly leaves and hooded flowers

SPECIES AND VARIETIES

Stachys Byzantina is one of those plants which you would have been almost certain to find in cottage gardens, usually grown as an edging plant. It produces dense mats of woolly grey leaves with magenta flowers in summer. There are a number of named varieties. 'Cotton Ball' is similar in many ways to the type plant with the exception that the flower spikes abort, producing cotton-like bobbles up the stems. 'Silver Carpet' was raised in Norfolk, and is a non-flowering variety with very attractive, evergreen, silvery foliage. Its low-growing habit makes it particularly effective as an edging to a path or border.

Stachys macrantha is another plant to have changed name, for years listed as *S. spicata*. It originates from the Caucasus, and over the years has been known by names other than the two mentioned here. The foliage is dark green, and downy to touch. In June, spikes of deep lilac flowers appear on 45cm/18in stems. 'Robusta' (AGM) is a particularly good choice, with lovely deep pink spikes on slightly shorter stems.

CULTIVATION

Soil type These plants will grow well in most well drained garden soils in either sun or lightly shaded areas.

Planting As with many hardy perennials, stachys can be planted in the autumn or spring.

Maintenance If in an exposed spot, *Stachys macrantha* may need some support in the way of twiggy sticks. The flowering spikes of *S. byzantina* are often removed, as it is grown principally for its foliage: the dead spikes soon become flabby and rather spoil the appearance of the plant. It also has a self-seeding habit which can become a nuisance. The centre of stachys can die out if not lifted and divided every three or so years.

Propagation Another easy plant to propagate by simply lifting and dividing. Select strong outer portions and replant immediately.

Pests and diseases Mildew can occasionally be a problem on the silvery leaved plant; control with a fungicide.

TRILLIUM

COMMON NAME: WAKE ROBIN
FAMILY: TRILLIACEAE

There are a number of trillium species available, all of them originating from the United States. These are very attractive woodland plants which flower in the spring.

SPECIES AND VARIETIES

Trillium grandiflorum (AGM), commonly known as wake robin, was introduced over 200 years ago. It is the best known species. They are fairly slow-growing, hardy herbaceous perennial plants which, left undisturbed, will form a sizable clump. In April the first of the pure white, three-petalled flowers open over mid-green foliage, in groups of three. There is a rare, lovely clear pink form, 'Roseum', and a gorgeous, pure white, double-flowered form, 'Flore Pleno' (AGM). *Trillium sessile* is another impressive plant, with handsome marbled foliage. The flowers are maroon and upright, with narrow, twisted petals. Well established plants growing in small groups are very eye-catching in the spring.

CULTIVATION

Soil type These require cool, moist, humus-rich conditions in a lightly shaded area. They will grow in more open positions provided they have sufficient moisture. Avoid heavy, poorly drained soils.

Planting For best effect the rhizomes should be planted 5cm/2in deep, ideally in groups. Planting can be done in the autumn or spring. Take care not to damage the fleshy tubers – once planted they should be left undisturbed.

Maintenance Take great care to avoid damaging these plants while in growth: if they are damaged, they will not regrow that season and this will, in turn, weaken the plant. Be careful not to disturb the roots when working around the plant. The foliage dies down in late summer, after which the site can be tidied up.

Propagation Lift the plants carefully in the autumn and divide, ensuring that

Trillium sessile; dark maroon flowers, requires a cool, moist, lightly shaded spot

each portion has at least one growing point. Avoid the temptation to divide into small sections, as they will take time to re-establish.

Pests and diseases These are plants which attract slugs and snails to the new growth in the spring – take precautions early (see Chapter 5, page 36).

VERBASCUM

COMMON NAME: MULLEIN
FAMILY: SCROPHULARIACEAE

These are stately border plants, with spikes of saucer-shaped flowers. They are sun lovers and will thrive in poor soils provided they are well drained.

SPECIES AND VARIETIES

Verbascum chaixii has grey green foliage which is woolly to the touch. The flower spike is at its best in June, reaching over 1m/3ft in height, with yellow flowers. There is also a white form listed simply as 'Album'.

One has only to glance through a hardy perennial specialist's catalogue to appreciate that there are many named varieties. One which attracted much attention when introduced was 'Helen Johnson' (AGM), with its spikes of brownish flowers. Another good choice is the light yellow 'Gainsborough' (AGM), also with yellow flowers. 'Cotswold Beauty' (AGM) has a purple centre. Others to look out for are the pure white 'Mont Blanc' and the deep rosy pink 'Pink Domino' (AGM).

CULTIVATION

Soil type Most well drained soils.

Planting Choose a sunny position and plant in the autumn or spring.

Verbascum; these tall, stately plants are commonly known as mullein

Maintenance The taller varieties may need support, especially if grown in rich soil. They are prolific self-seeders – removal of the flowering stem is advisable. In the autumn cut the plants down to ground level.

Propagation Verbascums are easily grown from seed; sow in the spring in a pan containing John Innes seed compost. Place in a frame and when large enough, prick out into a nursery bed. Plant seedlings into their flowering positions in the autumn. The named varieties do not come true from seed. Increase stock of these by taking 7cm/3in root cuttings in early spring. Root in an equal mix of peat and sand in a cold frame and, after they have produced three or more leaves, transfer to a nursery bed. Move to a permanent position in the autumn.

Pests and diseases Caterpillars of the mullein moth can quickly strip the foliage of verbascum. These caterpillars are easily seen and can be removed. Mildew is another problem but does not usually occur until flowering has finished. If seen, spray with fungicide.

ZANTEDESCHIA

COMMON NAMES: ARUM LILY, LILY OF THE NILE
FAMILY: ARACEAE

The exotic, moisture-loving *Zantedeschia aethiopica* is usually hardy in warmer areas but in colder districts, ample winter protection is required; alternatively lift and store under cover in the autumn. This stately plant will also grow in shallow water.

SPECIES AND VARIETIES

Zantedeschia aethiopica (AGM) is a deciduous species originating from South Africa. It forms a sizable clump of deep green, glossy, arrow-shaped leaves. The graceful, pure white spathes with yellow spadix are held well clear of the foliage on stems up to 90cm/36in in ideal conditions. The variety 'Crowborough' (AGM) is widely accepted as being the most reliable. Most forms are now regarded as having little to choose between them as far as reliability goes, provided they are protected during the winter months.

Zantedeschia aethiopica 'Crowborough'; widely regarded as being the most reliable form of this species, requires cool, moist soil

Among the varieties are 'White Sail' and 'Little Gem', both shorter than those mentioned. 'Green Goddess' (AGM) is different, having a green spathe with a white throat.

CULTIVATION

Soil type Moist, humus-rich soil.

Planting Choose a lightly shaded spot and plant in the spring, taking care not to damage the rhizomes.

Maintenance Remove dead flower spathes. If the plant is to remain in position during the winter, tidy up in the autumn and cover with straw, bracken or other material. In cold districts it is safest to lift and pot up in the autumn, overwintering in a frost-free greenhouse.

Propagation Divide the rhizomes in the spring and replant immediately.

Pests and diseases Viruses can attack the plant but zantedeschia are generally trouble free.

GARDENER'S GUIDE

HARDY PERENNIALS FOR ALKALINE CONDITIONS (LIME PRESENT)

Acanthus

Achillea

Alchemilla

Anemone

Artemisia

Aster

Bergenia

Campanula

Coreopsis

Delphinium

Doronicum

Echinops

Erigeron

Eryngium

Gypsophila

Helenium

Helleborus

Hemerocallis

Iris

Kniphofia

Lupinus

Nepeta

Papaver

Sedum

Solidago

Stachys

Acanthus spinosus

Aster amellus 'Vanity'

Bergenia 'Silberlicht' ('Silverlight')

Campanula persicifolia 'Caerulea Plena'

Eryngium alpinum

Hemerocallis 'Lark Song'

Papaver 'Glowing Embers'

Stachys macrantha 'Violacea'

HARDY PERENNIALS FOR FOLIAGE EFFECT

Ajuga

Alchemilla

Artemisia

Epimedium

Euphorbia

Hosta

Lamium

Liriope

Phlox 'Norah Leigh'

Pulmonaria

Rheum

Sedum

Artemisia schmidtiana 'Nana'

Euphorbia characias 'Spring Splendour'

Hosta fortunei var. *aureomarginata*

Lamium 'White Nancy'

WINTER-FLOWERING HARDY PERENNIALS (JANUARY–APRIL)

Bergenia

Brunnera

Caltha

Doronicum

Epimedium

Euphorbia

Helleborus

Paeonia mlokosewitschii

Primula vulgaris

Pulmonaria

Caltha palustris 'Flore Pleno'

Euphorbia griffithii 'Fireglow'

Paeonia mlokosewitschii

Helleborus

GLOSSARY

acid soil contains no free lime with pH of less than 6.5

annual a plant which grows and flowers in the same year and then dies

basal shoot from neck or crown of plant

biennial plant which completes growing cycle in two seasons

blotched petals with irregularly scattered colour patches

boss prominent centre stamens

cold frame an unheated box with sides of wood, plastic or brick and removable transparent top, used to protect plants from the cold

crown area of plant from which shoots and roots grow

cultivar cultivated variety

cutting portion of plant used for propagation

deadheading removal of dead flowers

division dividing plant for propagation

drill furrow in soil into which seeds are sown

evergreen retains foliage throughout winter

falls bottom petals on iris

fungicide product to treat mildew and rusts

ground cover low-growing ornamental plants useful for controlling weeds

grow on leave to grow until of a size suitable for planting out

humus organic matter in soil

hybrid plants raised from two species, varieties or cultivars

insecticide chemical product used to control insect pests

Rudbeckia 'Goldsturm' has prominent black bosses surrounded by bright yellow petals

The falls can be seen clearly in this picture of the tall bearded iris, *Iris* 'Pink Taffeta'

The variegated leaves of *Brunnera* 'Hadspen Cream' have a distinct cream edging

move on transfer to permanent positions

mulch bulky organic matter applied round plants to conserve moisture

perennial plants which grow and flower year after year

pH measure of acidity

pinch out to remove the growing tip

plant out to plant into permanent flowering positions

prick out to remove seedlings from the pot and space them out into trays, to allow an increase in size

propagator item of equipment for raising seedlings or rooting cuttings

raceme similar to a spike but with flowers on short stalks

reflexed petals that are bent back

rhizome horizontally growing, fleshy root

self-seeding a plant that scatters its seed naturally

spadix fleshy spike with small flowers

spathe bract surrounding flower

stopping taking out the growing tip to produce a more bushy plant

systemic insecticide which is absorbed by the plant and which travels in the sap

taken with a heel cutting taken to include a small portion of mature stem

tilth fine soil to sow seeds

transplant move from one place to another

umbel type of flower head

variegated leaves blotched, spotted or edged with a different colour

virus organism, for which there is no cure, causing malformation or discolouration

woody old mature portions of root

NAMING OF PLANTS

PLANTS are grouped, or classified, according to common characteristics. The names they are given indicate to which group they belong. The largest grouping, based on the structure of the plant's flowers, fruits and other organs, is the family. The family is then divided into genera and the genera into species. Every plant has a botanical name which is composed of two parts, the first indicating its genus and the second its species. Species may be further divided into subspecies.

Additional names indicate whether the subject is a hybrid (a cross between different genera or species), a cultivar (a man-made variation; the result of planned breeding), a variety (a naturally occurring variation as opposed to a man-made one) or a form (a plant with only a minor, but generally noticeable variation from the species). Series or groups are collections of hybrid cultivars of like parentage.

Many plants are known by two names, or have been known by another name in the past; to avoid confusion, these names may be given as synonyms. Common names (colloquial, everyday names) are also used.

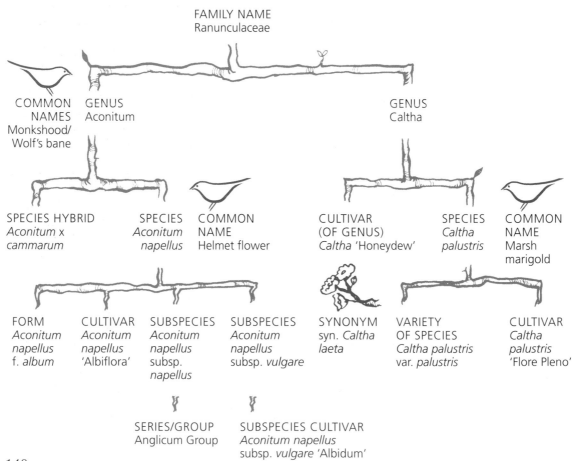

FAMILY NAME
Ranunculaceae

COMMON NAMES
Monkshood/
Wolf's bane

GENUS
Aconitum

GENUS
Caltha

SPECIES HYBRID
Aconitum x
cammarum

SPECIES
*Aconitum
napellus*

COMMON NAME
Helmet flower

CULTIVAR (OF GENUS)
Caltha 'Honeydew'

SPECIES
*Caltha
palustris*

COMMON NAME
Marsh
marigold

FORM
*Aconitum
napellus*
f. *album*

CULTIVAR
*Aconitum
napellus*
'Albiflora'

SUBSPECIES
*Aconitum
napellus*
subsp.
napellus

SUBSPECIES
*Aconitum
napellus*
subsp. *vulgare*

SYNONYM
syn. *Caltha
laeta*

VARIETY OF SPECIES
Caltha palustris
var. *palustris*

CULTIVAR
*Caltha
palustris*
'Flore Pleno'

SERIES/GROUP
Anglicum Group

SUBSPECIES CULTIVAR
Aconitum napellus
subsp. *vulgare* 'Albidum'

INDEX

Page numbers in **bold** refer to pictures.

INDEX OF CULTIVARS

Page numbers in **bold** refer to pictures.

ABOUT THE AUTHOR

PLANTS have been a part of my life from before my school days – my father worked as a head gardener. At the age of 16 my sizable and comprehensive collection of cushion-forming saxifrages, in those days known as the Kabschia type, attracted the attention of the local newspaper, and were featured on the front page.

On leaving school I worked for well-known nurserymen Wood & Ingram, until called up for National Service in the Royal Air Force. Back in civvy street I returned to gardening and gained experience not just in plants, but also in garden machinery, seeds and gardening products generally. Over the years I have enjoyed growing numerous types of plants including hardy perennials, chrysanthemums, bulbs, fuchsias, dahlias, and alpines, the latter three to show standard, successfully.

In the 1970s I began photographing plants and gardens. Wherever possible, I photograph plants in their natural habitat, including alpines in the Alps and other subjects in warmer climates. As a result, I have built up an extensive photographic library, with photos used in books and the magazine articles that I write for the national gardening press.

TITLES AVAILABLE FROM
GMC Publications

BOOKS

GARDENING

Auriculas for Everyone:
  How to Grow and Show Perfect Plants   *Mary Robinson*
Bird Boxes and Feeders for the Garden   *Dave Mackenzie*
The Birdwatcher's Garden   *Hazel & Pamela Johnson*
Companions to Clematis:
  Growing Clematis with Other Plants   *Marigold Badcock*
Creating Contrast with Dark Plants   *Freya Martin*

Gardening with Wild Plants   *Julian Slatcher*
Hardy Perennials: A Beginner's Guide   *Eric Sawford*
The Living Tropical Greenhouse: Creating a Haven
  for Butterflies   *John & Maureen Tampion*
Orchids are Easy: A Beginner's Guide
  to their Care and Cultivation   *Tom Gilland*
Plants that Span the Seasons   *Roger Wilson*

VIDEOS

Drop-in and Pinstuffed Seats   *David James*
Stuffover Upholstery   *David James*
Elliptical Turning   *David Springett*
Woodturning Wizardry   *David Springett*
Turning Between Centres: The Basics   *Dennis White*
Turning Bowls   *Dennis White*
Boxes, Goblets and Screw Threads   *Dennis White*
Novelties and Projects   *Dennis White*
Classic Profiles   *Dennis White*

Twists and Advanced Turning   *Dennis White*
Sharpening the Professional Way   *Jim Kingshott*
Sharpening Turning & Carving Tools   *Jim Kingshott*
Bowl Turning   *John Jordan*
Hollow Turning   *John Jordan*
Woodturning: A Foundation Course   *Keith Rowley*
Carving a Figure: The Female Form   *Ray Gonzalez*
The Router: A Beginner's Guide   *Alan Goodsell*
The Scroll Saw: A Beginner's Guide   *John Burke*

MAGAZINES

WOODTURNING ✦ WOODCARVING ✦ FURNITURE & CABINETMAKING
THE ROUTER ✦ WOODWORKING ✦ THE DOLLS' HOUSE MAGAZINE
WATER GARDENING ✦ EXOTIC GARDENING ✦ GARDEN CALENDAR
OUTDOOR PHOTOGRAPHY ✦ BUSINESSMATTERS

The above represents a selected list of titles currently published or scheduled to be published.
All are available direct from the Publishers or through bookshops, newsagents and specialist retailers.
To place an order, or to obtain a complete catalogue, contact:

GMC Publications
Castle Place, 166 High Street, Lewes, East Sussex BN7 1XU, United Kingdom
Tel: 01273 488005   Fax: 01273 478606   E-mail: pubs@thegmcgroup.com

Orders by credit card are accepted